PREPARING FOR A PROPERTY UPTURN

TRAPS AND PITFALLS IN REAL ESTATE INVESTMENTS

KU SWEE YONG

Marshall Cavendish
Business

Reprinted 2018

Published in 2017 by Marshall Cavendish Business
An imprint of Marshall Cavendish International

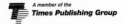

A member of the
Times Publishing Group

Other Marshall Cavendish Offices:
Marshall Cavendish Corporation. 99 White Plains Road, Tarrytown NY 10591-9001, USA • Marshall Cavendish International (Thailand) Co Ltd. 253 Asoke, 12th Flr, Sukhumvit 21 Road, Klongtoey Nua, Wattana, Bangkok 10110, Thailand • Marshall Cavendish (Malaysia) Sdn Bhd, Times Subang, Lot 46, Subang Hi-Tech Industrial Park, Batu Tiga, 40000 Shah Alam, Selangor Darul Ehsan, Malaysia

Marshall Cavendish is a registered trademark of Times Publishing Limited

National Library Board, Singapore Cataloguing-in-Publication Data

Name(s): Ku, Swee Yong.
Title: Preparing for a property upturn : trends and pitfalls in real estate investments / Ku Swee Yong.
Description: Singapore : Marshall Cavendish Business, [2017]
Identifier(s): OCN 1001516238 | ISBN 978-981-4779-91-3 (paperback)
Subject(s): LCSH: Real estate investment—Singapore. | Real estate investment—Singapore—Forecasting. | Real estate investment—Government policy—Singapore.
Classification: DDC 332.6324095957—dc23

Printed in Singapore by Fabulous Printers Pte Ltd

"In a time of deceit, telling the truth is a revolutionary act."

(A quote usually attributed to George Orwell,
but the exact source has not been determined.)

CONTENTS

PART 3: Developments in the Commercial Market

PART 4: From an Insider's Perspective

PART 5: Venturing Further Afield

PREFACE

The world has seen unprecedented and HUGE changes since I wrote the preface of my last book, *Weathering a Property Downturn*, in January 2016:

- UK decided to pull out of the European Union;
- Donald Trump became the President of the U.S.;
- Early initiatives of China's Belt & Road Initiative were realised, altering the trade, economic and political alignments of dozens of countries;
- Technology blowing winds of major disruptions;
- The world waking up to fake news; and
- Singapore standing at the crossroads of these changes.

What has not changed is my call on the Singapore property market: that prices will continue to trend down due to an abundance of floor space available that is not going to be matched by demand. My call for a downturn in the Singapore property market started in late 2013.

Being the first in the market to call the downturn, I was considered by most to be too bearish at that time. But my reading of the market has been spot on: the private residential price index has declined for 15 consecutive quarters since 3Q2013 and the total number of vacant private residences and Executive Condominiums increased by 73%, from 18,707 units in 3Q2013 to 32,419 units in 2Q2017.

The oversupply of space in the office, retail and industrial segments has also led to high vacancies and declining rentals in the last three years.

That vacancy is difficult to fill and will, in fact, expand given that job creation has gone negative in the first half of 2017. Singapore lost more than 17,000 jobs (excluding Foreign Domestic Workers) as the economy grapples with weakness in the Oil & Gas, Offshore & Marine and Construction industries, as well as having jobs made irrelevant by technology. If employment continues to contract, who will occupy these vacant homes?

In this book, I will elaborate on these upcoming problems and offer potential solutions.

As for my personal journey, the last one and a half years since publishing *Weathering a Property Downturn* have been a very fulfilling one. I had been on a learning journey, both as a student and as a teacher.

After being appointed by the Singapore Estate Agents Association (SEAA) to be a trainer for a course titled "Marketing of Overseas Properties in Singapore", I was required to attend a course to further qualify me as a trainer. As a part-time student, I found the Advanced Certificate for Training and Assessment (ACTA) course at the Institute for Adult Learning rather challenging. Having two very dedicated and well-qualified teachers, Mr Bryan Tan and Ms Loh Miew Ling, helped a lot. And I was fortunate to have nine very lively and clever classmates who contributed significantly to my learning: Denise Ng, Dorene Ng, Ellil Mathiyan, Ismail Hussien, Janet Chiew, Mike Ang, Paul Lee, Princeton Peters and Kogularam Naidu.

In the last year, I also had the honour to teach the Real Estate students in the National University of Singapore (NUS) and Ngee Ann Polytechnic (NP) as a part-time lecturer. Answering students' questions, thinking about how to get students to understand market research concepts and assessing whether they have learnt well are new challenges for me. Making the information and the sharing sessions meaningful for the students and getting them to relate the lectures to the real world is yet another set of challenges. Our teenagers and young adults have grown up to be fixated with "knowledge" and concepts that are misplaced or irrelevant in today's context.

For example, one misconception that should be broken in the minds of our young people is the old adage about real estate being the best hedge against inflation. This statement is true only if residential demand and supply are in balance, and everything else is kept constant (as the economists would say). In Singapore's current environment, vacant private residences and Executive Condominiums (ECs) number more than 33,000 islandwide and rentals are falling across all residential segments such as dormitories, HDB flats and private residences. Residential prices will continue to drop even while inflation climbs with healthcare, utilities, education and other costs.

I am particularly happy to be able to teach market analysis and research subjects in NUS and NP; helping the students to see the world differently from what our forefathers have taught us will allow them to survive better. The world is complex, and particularly so in this age of fake news and fake media.

Several articles in this book sought to dispel misconceptions and dissected other analysts' reports which I deemed misleading. While those opinion pieces and research reports did not amount to "fake news", many a time I could tell that the arguments were skewed, and that the opinions expressed could have been better substantiated.

For my teaching in NUS and NP, I also reference the good work of professors Carl T. Bergstrom and Jevin West from the University of Washington. They created a one-credit module (to be upgraded to four credits) for undergraduates in the university titled "Calling Bullshit in the Age of Big Data". On their course's website, the first statement to greet visitors is: "The world is awash with bullshit" and the professors claimed that they are "sick of it".

These professors subscribe to the following definition of bullshit: "Bullshit is language, statistical figures, data graphics, and other forms of presentation intended to persuade by impressing and overwhelming a reader or listener, with a blatant disregard for truth and logical coherence."

The objective of this course is to teach students "how to think critically about the data and models that constitute evidence in the social and natural sciences." Some of their teachings and materials that I shared with my students included: "spotting misleading axes", "spurious correlations" and "confusing causality with necessity or sufficiency".

Readers who are interested to learn more from this module may refer to www.callingbullshit.org for the full syllabus, lecture notes, recorded lectures and reading material.

I intend to remain a full-time property agent and I am thankful that on a part-time basis, I have the opportunity to journey on the path of learning and teaching.

I am grateful for the support of a team of undergraduates from the NUS Department of Real Estate, School of Design and Environment. They have assisted me with ground research, sieving through data and analysing market information. Most importantly, the debates and exchanges helped us to crystallise and refine our views about what the real estate market holds.

I would like to thank the following NUS undergraduates: Shannon Aw Qian Tong, Soh Yun Yee, Jolene Ng Hui Yi, Janice Chin Li Ping, Huang Shi Hui, Lee Sing Ying, Muhammad Izzat Afiq Bin Othman and David Chien Zhong Xin. In particular, Yun Yee is an A+ intern who played a major part in helping me with researching and analysing the housing market. I am also thankful for the research contribution of Ngee Ann Polytechnic graduate Justina Steven and current student Hui En Ni for the concept design of this book's cover.

I appreciate the generous sharing of knowledge and market data by industry partners: Andrew Goh Keng Hui from AGG (the "go-to guy" on HDB market), Gabriel Teo Hock Hoe, Feily Feilanny

Sofian, Shaw Yong Chee Chung, Colleen Lim Hui Shi and Nguon Chhayleang (a mini-authority on the Cambodian market); and partners in the Japan real estate market: Makoto "Micky" Kojima, Kouzo Kijima, Smica Create, RJC and Regalo Capital.

I am grateful for the encouragements from my teacher Mrs Toh Kah Beng, Luke Ng Kai Man from Century 21 Singapore, co-founders and partners from HugProperty.com Jeffery Sung Oon Hua, Winston Lam and Valerie Toh as well as the team from Marshall Cavendish, editors Melvin Neo and Sophia Susanto.

Finally, my deepest appreciation goes to my family and my colleagues in International Property Advisor Pte Ltd who had to put up with my grouchiness and long working hours. Without their support, my challenges would have been insurmountable.

Thank you all for helping me grow.

PART 1

LOOKING INTO
SINGAPORE'S FUTURE

1. Nearing the Edge of the Precipice: Ageing Population and the Housing Market

The article was co-authored with Jolene Ng Hui Yi and Soh Yun Yee, undergraduates from the Department of Real Estate, National University of Singapore.

Singapore citizens are ageing. We have rising life expectancy coupled with falling birth rates. Extrapolating the ageing trend points us to a few inevitabilities in the next 15 years:

- The demand for elderly healthcare will increase.
- The size of the Singaporean core workforce will reduce, resulting in a need for further automation, more foreign workers, or both.
- Baby boomers retiring from the workforce and passing away will lead to increased CPF withdrawals. However, there will be comparatively fewer young workers entering the workforce to contribute to CPF. The imbalance between funds redemption and funds contribution will likely lead to further amendments in CPF withdrawal limits and withdrawal ages.
- The retirement of about half a million baby boomers will cause some adjustments in the housing market. Some retirees will downsize or "right-size" their housing options, selling their larger homes to purchase or rent smaller homes while saving cash for retirement use (which may also affect consumption volumes and patterns).

- The passing on of the baby boomer generation will cause a seismic shift in the housing market due to a large increase in resale HDB flats.

The effects of our ageing population on housing prices are not yet prevalent today but are projected to be acute within the next 15 years. Let us take a deeper look into how the issue of our ageing population may affect the supply of HDB flats, against the backdrop of (a) a shrinking youth population, (b) a 90% home-ownership rate and (c) the current public housing policies.

International Academic Research

The effects of ageing population on the housing market of developed nations was discussed in a 2015 research article by Yumi Saita, Chihiro Shimizu and Tsutomu Watanabe from the Institute of Real Estate Studies (IRES), National University of Singapore, titled *Aging and Real Estate Prices: Evidence from Japanese and U.S. Regional Data*. The study concluded that property prices are negatively correlated with old age dependency ratio, i.e. property prices will decline when there are proportionately more senior citizens than youths.

This school of thought has been around since as early as 1989, and it was initiated by Gregory Mankiw and David Weil from Harvard University. In an article titled *The Baby Boom, the Baby Bust, and the Housing Market*, the authors examined the impact of major demographic changes on the housing market in the United States. They suggested that housing demand growth will slow down over time as baby boomers grow older and the baby bust generation enters the housing purchase scene. Hence, housing prices are bound to decline over time due to the ageing population.

The research by Mankiw and Weil was well ahead of its time. Another paper published in *The Annals of the American Academy* in November 2009 by Dowell Myers and John Pitkin from the University of Southern California reached a similar conclusion. Myers and

Pitkin considered "the impacts of the sell-off of housing by the aging of the massive baby boom generation that is anticipated to take place beginning in 2020 and discuss whether the expected housing glut can be absorbed by a relatively smaller and less advantaged younger generation in the 2040s."

Similarly, a publication in 2010 titled *Population Ageing and House Prices in Australia* by Ross Guest and Robyn Swift from Griffith University, Australia, also reached similar conclusions. It suggested that the ageing population in Australia may cause real housing prices to be lower than they would otherwise be, a difference of 3–20% between the year 2008 and 2050.

The Ageing Population and Increasing Death Rate

For Singapore, the Population White Paper published by the National Population and Talent Division in January 2013 had projected our old age support ratio to decline from 5.9 in 2012 to 2.1 in 2030. Old age support ratio is a measure that refers to the proportion of residents aged 20–64 (considered to be in their economically productive age) per resident aged 65 years and over (considered to be retired and therefore requires support from those who are economically active).

Singapore will not be spared from the pressures that an ageing population adds to our housing market. Furthermore, we believe that this issue should take on a higher concern for Singapore than Japan, the U.S. or Australia as the majority of our citizen population owns a HDB flat.

Death is inevitable. When Singaporean baby boomers pass away, their HDB flats may be inherited by their children. But we believe that for most cases, their children are not able to inherit the flats due to concurrent ownership of residential properties. Their flats will be sold in the resale market to other eligible buyers. The problems will not be severe if the supply of resale flats due to death can be absorbed by a sizable pool of demand from younger families.

Figure 1: Singapore Citizens' Population Pyramid 2016

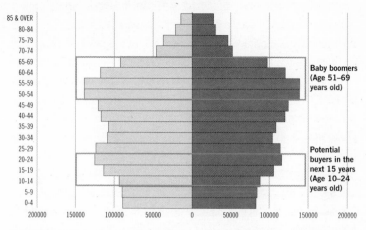

Citizen Population by Age Groups and Sex, Jun 2016

Source: Singstat, IPA

Figure 2: Number of deaths of citizens aged 51 years and above today over the next 15 years

Year*	Total number of deaths of citizen in the baby boomers generation in each 5 year period*	Average number of deaths of citizens per year**
2017- 2021	132,148	26,430
2022- 2026	147,510	29,502
2027- 2031	165,761	33,152

*Analysis is done in intervals of five years as official sources only publish population numbers grouped in bands of five years.

**Calculated from Singapore resident death rate and citizen population numbers updated as of June 2016. As the authorities do not publish data on "citizen death rate", we approximated the resident death rate as the citizen death rate.

Source: Singstat, IPA

However, given the falling birth rates in the last 20 years, we predict that the future demand for resale HDB flats will be increasingly insufficient to absorb the escalating resale supply caused by the deaths of baby boomers.

To begin, let us examine the demographics of the citizen population in 2016. More than 25% of the citizen population[1] are post-war baby boomers, aged 51 to 69 years old today, who will retire from the workforce and enter their silver years by 2031[2]. The baby boomers population accounts for the bulk of the citizen population, reflected by the large bulge in the population pyramid in Figure 1.

In 2016 alone, about 13,500 citizens aged 65 and over passed away.[3] Over the next 15 years, there will be a gradual increase in the annual number of deaths of citizens from the baby boomers generation and older. From Figure 2, we see that the average number of deaths of citizens will increase from 26,430 per year between 2017 and 2021, to 29,502 per year between 2022 and 2026. The average numbers of deaths of citizens aged 65 and above will reach a high of 33,150 per year in 2031, about two and a half times the number in 2016.

Increase in Resale Flats due to Deaths of Owners

The HDB housing programme was ramped up quickly in the 1970s and 1980s to cater for the large population of baby boomers. HDB completed more than 550,000 flats in that period, i.e. about 27,500 flats per year (see Chapter 2). Supported by a major drive for home ownership and the use of CPF funds, the percentage of Singaporean families living in HDB flats shot up from 35% in 1970 to 87% in 1990.

We believe that the passing away of baby boomers will create a large supply of resale HDB flats, causing significant downward pressure on prices.

We made enquiries with HDB about the number of death-related-resale HDB flats in the past five years from 2012 to 2016. However, this statistic is not tracked. We also tried surveying property agents who are actively transacting HDB flats[4] and asked if they have dealt with resale cases which were the result of beneficiaries having to sell the flat after their parents or siblings have passed away.

Our own estimate is that there are probably 200 to 500 of such cases every year in the last few years. However, since there is no official data, we will assume that the number of HDB flats put up in the resale market resulting from death is negligible. The numbers are small today because while there are HDB owners passing away, most of them leave behind their spouses who continue to hold on to the HDB flats.

However, looking forward into the next 15 years, we estimate that the number should increase significantly in tandem with the rise in the number of baby boomer deaths (see Figure 2), to more than 8,000 cases per year in the five-year period of 2027–2031.

To put the numbers into perspective, the cumulative resale transactions for the past five years from 2012 to 2016 was a total of 102,755, that is, an average of 20,551 resale transactions per year.

Figure 3: Number of HDB flats projected to be released into the resale market due to death of owners in the next 15 years

Year*	Number of HDB flats released due to deaths in each 5-year-period*	Number of HDB flats released due to deaths per year in each period*
2012–2016	Negligible	Negligible
2017–2021	5,137	1,027
2022–2026	17,711	3,542
2027–2031	40,592	8,118

Analysis is done in intervals of five years as Singstat only releases population numbers by age group in bands of five years.

**Number of HDB flats released takes into account resale supply resulting from death only*

Source: Singstat, IPA

---

[1] Citizen population comprises people who hold Singapore citizenship; Resident population comprises Singapore citizens and Permanent Residents (PR); Total population comprises citizens, PR and non-residents or foreigners who are here for work, study or family reasons.

[2] "Retiree households" are defined as those comprising solely non-working persons aged 60 years and over. Note that old age support ratio uses 65 years of age while 'retiree' is defined from 60 years of age.

[3] Calculated by applying the resident death rate on citizen population numbers published as of June 2016. There will be a slight discrepancy as "residents refer to citizens and PRs". The authors were puzzled when informed by Singstat that "data on citizen death rates are not available".

[4] As property agents ourselves, and amongst our agent-partners, we know that there are transactions of death-related-resale flats. But perhaps due to a fear that the HDB flat might have to be sold at a discount to the market price, very few cases were identified as death-related-resale.

This implies that the average demand for resale flats, assuming that transactions are maintained at this level, is 20,551 a year. Death related cases, at 8,118 a year, will add about 40% to the resale supply! That degree of increase in supply will surely put significant pressure on resale prices.

While the number of new flats released by the HDB can be controlled, the supply of resale flats is something that policymakers have little control over. More senior citizens are bound to pass away in the next 15 years, resulting in a large supply of HDB flats for sale in the market.

Why Do Children of the Deceased Not Inherit the Flats?

To answer those questions, we have to look into the rules and regulations surrounding HDB "ownership", or long-term-lease, in Singapore. Firstly, only Singapore citizens and Singapore PRs are eligible to own HDB flats. PRs are further restricted to purchase a HDB flat only after obtaining the PR status for three years or more. Secondly, in a transfer of HDB flat ownership, any individual already in possession of a HDB flat will not be eligible to inherit the flat of the deceased[5] as HDB flat owners are not allowed to own two residential properties at one time. To own an inherited HDB flat, the existing residential property under the name of the proposed owner, regardless of private or public housing, must be disposed of within six months of inheriting the flat.

However, if certain eligibility conditions are met, a private residential owner may inherit a HDB flat provided the family lives in that HDB flat. Amongst the conditions are citizenship, family nucleus and whether the flat was a non-subsidised flat leased before 30 August 2010.[6]

We feel that the policies are getting complicated with many conditions and exceptions. Perhaps these policies on inheritance of flats might get even more complicated as Singaporeans age further. But for now, based on the existing policies, we estimate that there will not be sufficient families that can inherit HDB flats from their deceased family members, so the resale supply will increase strongly.

Firstly, home ownership is already at 90% in Singapore, ranking us amongst the highest in the world. For the past 20 years, the home-ownership rate has been fluctuating around the 90% level, meaning that despite the government's push for higher home-ownership rates, we have reached a ceiling for the number of households who can afford to and who want to own their homes.

Secondly, 80% of Singapore households live in HDB flats. From the report HDB Key Statistics 2016 and SingStat's data we know that 92.2% of the roughly 1.0 million HDB flats are owned (on 99-year right-of-use lease term).

Add the above statistics together, and we can see that it is highly probable that children of the baby boomer generation are already owners of HDB flats. Under the current rules, when the baby boomers pass on, these children who already own HDB flats cannot inherit the flats and therefore, one of the flats will be available in the resale market.

When more than 8,000 *additional* flats per year are available in the resale market in 2031, will there be sufficient demand from young first-time buyers to support the volume?

Fewer and Fewer Young and New Families to Buy Flats

The worry looms as we see that the supply of resale HDB flats way surpasses demand. We first identify the younger population of aged 25 to 29 years old as the main drivers for housing demand in each five-year interval[7] from today. Citizens in this age group have already built up some savings and are most likely to be seeking their matrimonial homes and embarking on family life. They will therefore

---

[5] Provided that this individual is an immediate family member of the deceased, eg. spouse, parents, child, sibling.

[6] Reference HDB website : http://askhdb.hdb.gov.sg/Themes/HDB/Answers.aspx?MesId=1 5656392&From=Show&TOPV=YES&VMesID=4823244

[7] Citizens are grouped in age-cohorts of 5 years, analysis can only be best done based on 5-year-intervals instead of yearly intervals.

Figure 4: Total estimated number of citizens turning 25–29 years old in the years 2021, 2026 and 2031 based on the citizen population tree in 2016 shown in Figure 1.

Total estimated number of citizens entering the 25–29 years old age group					
Age Group \ Year	2016	2021	2026	2031	Increase in number of people entering the 25–29 years old age group after 2016 and into 2031:
10-14	181,745	-	-	-	
15-19	219,247	181,708	-	-	
20-24	242,395	219,107	181,663	-	
25-29	238,534	**242,228**	**219,041**	**181,608**	**642,877**

*Calculated based on resident death rate and citizen population numbers updated as of June 2016. Does not take into account the number of new PRs and Singapore citizenships granted.

Source: Singstat, IPA

form the fresh pool of demand for the resale flats, and new flats, each year.

However, the population numbers of these cohorts are way smaller than the baby boomers'.

It can be seen in Figure 4 that the number of Singapore citizens aged 25 to 29 will be shrinking over the next 15 years, consequently, the demand for HDB flats will be proportionately lower. Extrapolating the population tree and taking into account resident death rates, we estimate that the cohort size of Singapore citizens aged 25 to 29 will shrink from 238,534 in 2016 to 181,608 in 2031. Furthermore, between 2016 and 2031, there will be a total of 642,877 citizens who will grow into and beyond the 25 to 29 years' home-buying age. However, not all citizens in that age group will purchase a resale HDB flat as they may also opt to purchase *new* HDB flats, private residential properties or executive condominiums.

In addition, of those who have the financial ability to purchase a HDB flat, only a proportion will be eligible. Under the rules and regulations, only married couples can purchase a HDB flat, while singles will only be eligible at the age of 35. Hence, considering the above points, the demand for resale HDB flats from citizens aged 25–29 will only be a fraction of their total population.

The decline in the number of younger citizens further hints at an imbalance in supply and demand, which puts us at a danger of falling off a rocky cliff. As supply surges, we will simultaneously be met with a steepening drop in the number of younger citizens capable and eligible to absorb the available resale flats.

Increased Supply with Lower Demand as We Approach 2031

The pressure from additional death-related resale supply will build up over the next 10 to 15 years. At the same time, demand will reduce due to a shrinking youth population. The widening gap between supply and demand will lead to a decline in resale HDB values. Although we are unable to accurately forecast when the steepening decline of prices will begin, it is inevitable that HDB flat prices will drop over the next 15 years if economic conditions and housing policies remain the same.

And to compound the price decline: ageing HDB flats. The price declines of old HDB flats steepens from the point of 40 years' age and by 2030, more than 400,000 HDB flats will be older than 40 years, i.e. 400,000 flats will be left with leases of 59 years or less. The point about the price depreciation of old HDB flats will be elaborated in the next chapter.

How Do We Compare with Japan?

Japan's ageing population and its impact on housing prices are highlighted in the IRES paper. We may apply the same arguments to Singapore. However, our situation is far more challenging.

Home-ownership rate in Singapore at 90.9%[8] is much higher than that in Japan at 61.9%[9]. In view of the policies restricting Singaporeans from owning two HDB flats and our very high rate of public housing ownership, it means that as more people pass away, more flats will be sold. On the other hand, Japan does not have any of these constraints.

---

[8] This includes public and private housing. Reference: Population Trends 2016, SingStat.
[9] Japan's home-ownership rate updated as of 2013. 2016 data is not available as it is computed every five years.

Furthermore, public housing in Japan is not owned by individuals but rented out and managed by a government agency known as the Urban Renaissance Agency. If a tenant passes away, the Japanese government simply lets out the home to another tenant. In Singapore, public housing accounts for 71.4% of the total residential stock and 92.2%[10] of that are owned.

As HDB accounts for a large proportion of the total residential stock in Singapore, HDB housing prices form the low-end benchmark for private residential values. In other words, a decline in HDB housing prices will have an indirect impact on private residential values. This issue is not applicable to Japan.

Changes to Public Housing Policies Needed

So how do we counter the effects of the passing baby boomers pressuring down on our public housing values?

Firstly, it should be eminently clear now that the current citizen population will not be enough to support the housing market in the long term. Therefore, allowing immigrants to become PRs and subsequently obtain citizenship status is important since only Singaporeans and PRs can purchase HDB flats. The population growth will absorb some of the resale HDB flat supply. However, to ensure that there will be a sustainable stream of immigrants, the economy must stay strong and Singapore must remain attractive with an abundance of well-paying jobs. This may not be an easy feat given the uncertainties in Singapore's ability to adapt to rapid technological changes and shifts in the global environment. This point will be further elaborated in the chapter discussing Singapore's concept plan for the next 50 years.

Secondly, we can loosen HDB ownership rules such as allowing ownership of two HDB flats instead of one and allow all newly minted PRs to purchase HDB flats. However, there is a downside to this move. While the excess supply will be purchased and owned, they do not necessarily mean that there will be occupants. Individuals owning two flats may rent one out for passive income, but if we are unable to create many more jobs, finding a tenant will be an issue and the flats will be left vacant.

Thirdly, in death-related and inheritance resale cases, we suggest that the HDB offers family members an option where HDB takes possession of these flats at prevailing resale prices. Through this method, HDB can increase its stock of rental flats and offer the public more housing choices. This may increase the occupancy of flats while providing affordable rental flats for low-income families, including for three-room to five-room flats as opposed to mainly one-room or two-room flats today. Other rental schemes can also be further explored such as operating the excess flats as hostels if they are near to schools, short-term rentals, retirement housing, etc. However, this requires a large government budget to be set aside.

Lastly, HDB could consider limiting the supply of new flats. Extending the suggestion above, HDB could purchase the resale flat when its final owner-occupier has passed on, refurbish it and then sell it under the Sale of Balance Flats Scheme today.

Conclusion

The ageing population in Singapore will be no different to Japan's and other developed countries, except that we have the highest home-ownership rate amongst these countries.

It is not too early to start considering how the rapidly ageing population will cause home prices to decline. We are relatively certain that this issue will balloon in size within the next 15 years.

HDB resale prices will soon decline as the escalating supply of resale flats resulting from an increased number of citizens passing away and having to dispose of their HDB flats, and the decreasing number of younger residents who will be able to purchase them. The decline will be gradual but the speed will certainly accelerate as shown in the numbers in Figures 1, 2 and 3.

---

[10] There around 1 million HDB flats in 2016 and more than 900,000 flats are "owned" by resident families, while the rest are retained by the HDB for renting to the lower income families.

Furthermore, as the 99-year lease tenure continues to shorten, value will depreciate, which will compound the price decline. We estimate that more than 400,000 HDB flats will have a remaining lease of less than 59 years by 2031, i.e. many of the resale flats will be old and of lower value. The increasing number of old flats will add pressure to push housing prices downwards.

However, there may still be light before the end of the tunnel if public awareness of this issue is improved. Senior citizens, whose children already own HDB flats, should be informed of the option to sell their flats before they pass away to avoid the urgency of sale. This will help ease selling pressures as we approach 2031 and decline in housing prices may be more gradual as a result.

Singapore had for a long time been basking in her uniqueness of having one of the highest home-ownership rates in the world today. It may be the time we rethink our housing policies and adjust our plans for the future.

Authors' Note

We recognise that HDB flats are not owned and are instead merely on long-term lease. But for the ease of comprehension in this article, we use terms such as "HDB owners" instead of "HDB lessees".

2. Facing the 99-Year Leasehold Chasm of Public Housing

The article was co-authored with Soh Yun Yee, an undergraduate from the Department of Real Estate, National University of Singapore.

A particular concern about the future of housing prices has recently raised eyebrows and sparked discussions in the mainstream media — it is about the expiring 99-year leases of HDB flats. It was started by an article published by *Lianhe Zaobao* on 15 March 2017. It highlighted the increasing number of old HDB flats that transacted at high prices over the last three years. It cited examples of flats of over 40 years of age that transacted at eye-popping prices: a three-room HDB flat at $708,000 and five-room flats at nearly a million dollars. The discussion took traction when the Minister for National Development (MND), Mr Lawrence Wong, commented on it through a post on the MND blog on 24 March 2017.

In particular, the Minister addressed the widely held opinion of buying a very old HDB flat in the hope of getting a windfall gain through the Selective En bloc Redevelopment Scheme (SERS). He reminded all HDB owners and prospective buyers: "Please do not assume that all old HDB flats are automatically eligible for SERS."[1]

---

[1] Source: https://mndsingapore.wordpress.com/2017/03/24/choosing-a-home-for-life/

Figure 1: Number of HDB dwelling units constructed in each 10 year period between 1960 and 2020 (estimated).

Includes DBSS Flats of 616 units for 2006–2010, and 8,034 units for 2011–2015.

Source: HDB, IPA

To put the numbers in perspective, we have about 70,000 flats which are more than 40 years old, and 280,000 flats which are between 30 and 40 years of age. Consider the number of old flats and the land required for building new flats to rehouse residents from these old flats. And then consider the financial commitment required for that rehousing exercise. Say for the above 350,000 old flats, we embarked on 20 years of SERS exercise starting from the year 2040 to the year 2060. We will need 17,500 additional flats per year for relocation. If the replacement of each old HDB flat and the residents' relocation to a new flat cost the government $200,000, including construction costs and other grants, the budget required will be $3.5 billion a year for 20 years!

No surprises then, that amongst the list of issues to consider, the Minister highlighted that SERS is possible only when the government has the financial resources to carry out such a program.

Hence, buyers should not make hasty decisions, thinking that all old HDB flats will be redeveloped. The reality is that the value of the flats will decline rapidly along with the depreciation near the end of the 99-year lease.

Buyers of old flats gave other reasons for buying. These include the merit of living in a larger flat and the wish to live in close proximity to their parents. To enlighten the public on the depreciation of HDB flats' value, an article in the *Straits Times* titled *Will you still love your HDB flat when it's over 64?* appeared on 12 April 2017. We provided a visual illustration of the decline of HDB flats' prices over a 56-year time horizon, using a high-priced old flat in Marine Parade as an example.

How might old HDB flats depreciate in value?

In general, when considering the value of old HDB flats, we need to take into account:

- the value of using the flat (also known as the utility value, which may be related to rental value),
- the financing available for the flat (as it has a direct correlation to the number of people who can afford it), and
- the CPF money that can be used to pay for it (as it affects the cashflow of the owners who have CPF funds).

In the case of private residential properties, there is another consideration: replacement value, or the potential value of en bloc sales. But this is not applicable to HDB flats as "HDB owners" are merely long-term tenants.

Property buyers will be able to fund their HDB flats with either a bank loan, a HDB loan, CPF money or cash. However, this is only applicable when the property is between 0 and 64 years old (i.e. remaining lease of between 99 to 35 years). When the remaining lease on the HDB flat is 65 years or less, the shorter bank loan tenures available to buyers of the resale flats begin to limit the number of buyers in the market who would consider these flats. We consider this the first tipping point. But this is obviously not a big deterrent given that so many old flats are still transacting at "high

Figure 2 The value of HDB flats depreciates at a significantly faster pace as the age of the flat exceeds 40 years.

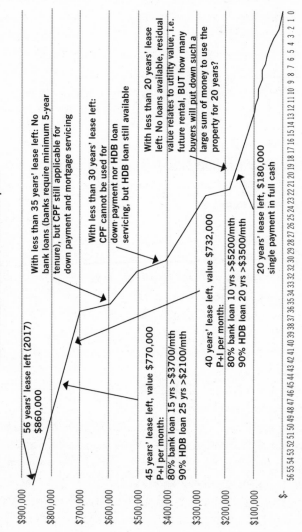

Mature Estate HDB five-room flat price

56 years' lease left (2017)
$860,000

With less than 35 years' lease left: No bank loans (banks require minimum 5-year tenure), but CPF still applicable for down payment and mortgage servicing

With less than 30 years' lease left: CPF cannot be used for down payment nor HDB loan servicing, but HDB loan still available

45 years' lease left, value $770,000
P+I per month:
80% bank loan 15 yrs >$3700/mth
90% HDB loan 25 yrs >$2100/mth

With less than 20 years' lease left: No loans available, residual value relates to utility value, i.e. future rental, BUT how many buyers will put down such a large sum of money to use the property for 20 years?

40 years' lease left, value $732,000
P+I per month:
80% bank loan 10 yrs >$5200/mth
90% HDB loan 20 yrs >$3500/mth

20 years' lease left, $180,000
single payment in full cash

Source: IPA

prices". However, as the remaining lease drops further, we see the other tipping points follow (see Figure 2).

The value of HDB flats will shrink at a faster pace when left with 35 years of lease — this is the second tipping point of the downward ride in prices. This drop occurs because banks normally require a minimum loan tenure of five years and no loans will be available for properties with leftover leases of 30 years or less. This leaves the buyers with getting a HDB loan (a maximum of 15 years at this point), or to use CPF and/or cash for full payment.

Banks are more inclined to provide loans if buyers are eligible to use their CPF funds for the loan repayments as it is deemed to be less risky to the lenders. The CPF Board determines if one is eligible "based on the sum of the age of the applicant and the remaining lease on the property". For example, if the buyer is 35 years old and the property is left with 40 years of lease, the buyer will not be eligible. However, any sum of "the age of applicant and remaining lease" above 80 will be deemed eligible. In fact, the CPF policies restrict younger buyers from owning old properties that have a short remaining lease so that these buyers will not be holding properties that have leases expiring when they are still alive.

The third tipping point comes when there is 30 years of lease remaining, CPF funds will no longer be allowed for down payment nor for HDB loan servicing. A HDB loan, serviced solely with cash will be the only financing option that remains. However, this loan will have to be repaid within 10 years and is also under the condition that the remaining lease of the property covers the buyer up to 80 years old or more. The monthly repayment of principal plus interest on the HDB loan over a short period means that the monthly cash outlay may be rather prohibitive, unless the flat was sold at a low price of say below $200,000.

The fourth tipping point is when the remaining leases drop to 20 years and under. Buyers will not be eligible for any loans and CPF funds cannot be used for the purchase. All transactions must be fully paid with cash upfront. Consider this: how many families would have the ability to pay up a large sum of cash, say $100,000, in order to lease an old flat that will depreciate to zero value within 20 years? The number of potential buyers in this category will be small. Therefore prices should decline quickly from here on.

Let us revisit the example illustrated in Figure 1. The buyer paid $860,000 for the 43-year-old five-room flat. 56 years left on the lease in 2017. Assuming that the flat is in good physical condition when he wants to sell it in the year 2033, with 40 years of lease left and its price falls at 1% a year, it would be valued at $732,000 then.

If rules do not change, a buyer can only get a bank loan with a 10-year tenure to finance the flat, or an HDB loan with a 20-year tenure. For a bank loan, the monthly mortgage payment will be $5,200 (for an 80% loan over 10 years) and $3,500 for an HDB loan (a 90% loan over 20 years). How many households would have sufficient income to qualify for a mortgage that requires a monthly repayment of $5,200? Furthermore, households can opt to purchase newer flats with longer leases and take loans with longer durations and lower monthly mortgages. This makes old resale flats even less attractive to purchase.

In fact, we have been too optimistic about the slope of the decline in Figure 2. The small number of families willing to buy very old properties with say less than 35 years remaining lease and all the limited funding options that go with it, means that the drop at Tipping Point 2 should be more severe than what is depicted here.

At every tipping point, there will be a decreasing pool of prospective buyers who possess the financial abilities to purchase. There will also be fewer buyers who will find the purchase worthwhile compared to paying monthly rentals over the long term.

The Minister's post on the MND Blog reminded Singaporeans that the value of HDB flats will go to zero if they were not picked for SERS. And that apparently caused a groundswell of concern. While keyboard warriors on social media did not seem to take much heed about this subject, journalists from several mainstream media followed up on the subject.

On 12 April 2017, the Minister followed up on the discussion with a Facebook post, reassuring all that HDB flats remain a good store of asset value for future retirement needs[2]. He explained that with careful planning and considerations, it is still possible for HDB flat owners to encash their property. Methods include right-sizing and adopting the Lease Buyback Scheme (LBS). The latter will result in lesser cash but it will allow home owners to continue staying in it. Another *Straits Times* article titled *To buy an old HDB flat or not, that is the question* heaped praises of Mr Wong's response and advice. The article further suggested that buyers who expect returns from the resale of the property should buy properties that are less than 20 years old and not those of 30 or 40 years of age.

However, the Minister missed out the fact that the total number of old flats will only increase with time if existing policies remain unchanged. The hard truth that HDB flats will depreciate to an eventual zero value remains, and HDB owners must come to terms with it.

Furthermore, the Minister began his Facebook post with the statement "HDB flats, like many private properties, are sold on a 99-year lease." The public spotted two errors within this statement of 12 words: (1) that HDB flats are not sold, merely leased, and (2) the 99-year lease of a HDB flat is unlike the 99-year lease of private properties. (Side note: it is interesting to read the comments below the Minister's post to see what Singaporeans say about this topic.)

The issues related to the lease decay of leasehold properties do not only affect HDB flats, other types of leasehold properties such as offices, retail shops, factories and private residences depreciate over time too. The problem is simply more acute for HDB flats as the

---

[2] https://web.facebook.com/LawrenceWongST/photos/a.194878853886799.37834.19213 0117495006/1440467345994604/?type=3&theater

owners only possess the right to use the flats and the property title and ownership remain with HDB. Owners do not have the autonomy to decide on what happens to their property as the leases run down. In contrast, owners of, for example, private residences, possess the strata title to their living space. Hence, they have a collective sales market wholly dependent on the decision of the majority of the property owners and the availability of developers willing to buy en bloc to redevelop.

Various discussions in the mainstream and social media gave the public an awakening from their lofty dreams of endlessly profiting from the HDB flats they thought they owned. Having woken up to the possible monetary loss in reselling old flats with short leases, many individuals suggested ways to justify the value of old flats. An example, based on a calculation where the price per square foot and the remaining years of lease, was proposed in the *Straits Times* article *How to figure out if an old HDB flat is worth its asking price* on 8 April 2017.

A Bukit Timah HDB flat was taken as an example. The flat of 1,345 sqft was sold for $950,000 in 2017 translating to a unit price of $706 per sqft. That flat was built in 1974 on a 99-year lease (i.e remaining 56 years on the lease) and hence, the price per sqft per annum remaining is $12.60. The author has suggested this as a simple method that allows for easy comparisons between other properties in the vicinity. In this case, the HDB flat is compared to a 1,271 sqft unit in High Oak condominium nearby that was sold in December 2016 for $995,000 or $783 per sqft. With 78 years left, it translates to $10 per sqft per annum. The author concluded that the condominium would be a better buy than the HDB flat as it is priced at a lower per sqft per annum amount, is newer and also comes with facilities.

However, the above calculation only focuses on the depreciation of a property. An alternative calculation that compares the costs of ownership and the costs of use as a tenant if one were to rent instead of buy, would allow for a better decision. Let us use the flat mentioned in Figure 2 as an example and assume that it sells at $770,000 with 45 years lease remaining. The costs of ownership include the depreciation of the flat, loan interest expenses, service and conservancy charges (S&CC) and property taxes (yes, even though all HDB flats are owned by the HDB, flat "owners" need to pay property taxes). Buyers also fail to earn the CPF interests when CPF monies are withdrawn for upfront payments and monthly loan repayments for the purchase.

For a start, depreciation of the flat can be assumed to be linear and hence, approximately $17,110 annually (or $1,425 monthly). The other costs can then be added up to the depreciation and the total compared to rental prices in the neighbourhood. If the flat can be rented at a lower price than the total costs of ownership, it would be more economical to rent.

Furthermore, an advantage of renting would be that the large sum of upfront capital that would otherwise be spent in the HDB flat purchase can be invested wisely. The various long term costs involved in owning a flat may be opportunity costs to individuals as investing the money in other ways may result in positive returns as opposed to expenses down the drain.

Other suggestions

Some other solutions have been offered to alleviate the situation of HDB flats depreciating to zero value at the end of their lease. The most common suggestion is for the government to allow lease extensions. A *Straits Times* article titled *HDB leases and what's in store for retirement as society ages* was published on 15 April 2017. It compiled several examples of how other countries deal with expiring land leases: China allows properties with 70-year leases to be renewed unconditionally; Hong Kong allows an extension of leases for 50 years without having to pay any additional lease extension charges; Britain allows eligible flat owners and landed house owners to extend leases by 90 years and 50 years respectively, at a cost pegged to market rates.

Allowing for lease extensions would work if the government does not have alternative uses for the land. The quality of the HDB flats must be built to a standard that allows for leases to be extended. We do not think that these conditions exist for HDB flats. Furthermore, the cost of maintaining century-old flats may be significant as the physical obsolescence of a building is inevitable with age.

Another suggestion to prevent prices from dropping too fast at Tipping Point 1 and Tipping Point 2 would be to allow CPF funds and loans to be used for flats with remaining leases of less than 30 years. The number of prospective flat buyers will be bigger and the decline in resale flat prices may be more gradual.

However, this is merely kicking the can down the road. Allowing CPF funds and loans to be used for such old flats will result in even more losses for the families involved. For a retiree whose longevity might outlast the remaining lease of the HDB flat, his retirement fund will be wiped out when the lease hits the big zero.

Figure 3: Most buyers think that HDB flat prices will surely go up in the foreseeable future. In that case, the price graph may follow the dashed line. But eventually, the value will still drop to zero.

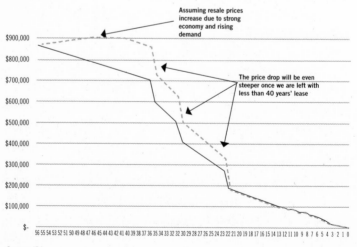

Source: IPA

Our proposal: To completely prevent HDB flat owners from shouldering the risk of losing their money on a depreciating asset, we suggest that HDB consider taking on the role of the "market maker" for public residential properties.

HDB can fix the price-formula for buying back flats from lessees by basing the future value of the flats on lease depreciation, inflation rate, GDP growth rate, and household income growth rate.

This way, a new HDB lessee buying a flat today will know the value of his HDB flat if he sells it in, say, the year 2040. The price can be fixed into a formula such as:

> Price in 2040 = Today's purchase price – depreciation of X% – Inflation factor + GDP growth factor + Household income growth factor

By using the word "factor" we mean to say the cumulative inflation (or depreciation or GDP growth or household income growth/decline as the case may be) over the period from today till 2040.

Although the price-formula is fixed at the time of entering into a contract with the HDB, the price-formula may be tweaked for buyers in 2018 or 2025 as and when the HDB feels that the formula needs to be adjusted. The adjusted formula will only apply forward, to new HDB lessees from that point onwards.

In this scheme, prospective HDB owners will buy and sell properties directly with HDB. The buy-price and sell-price will be quoted in a transparent manner, with a spread that can cover the costs and profits for HDB. Thus, the HDB becomes the market maker.

This is unlike the Lease Buyback Scheme (where a part of the lease is sold back to HDB) which, although allowing retirees to cash in on their homes earlier, creates an entirely different set of issues that have to be dealt with in future.

In addition, with HDB as the market maker, SERS can also be eliminated. When the lease of a flat runs down and the flats' physical condition deteriorate, property owners may choose to sell it back to HDB and purchase a new flat or a resale flat from the HDB. In the interim, HDB can lease the units out until every flat lessee in the block had sold their flats back to HDB. Then the block is ready for redevelopment.

In this case, there will not be a need to pay for the cost of SERS, in contrast to the current arrangement where residents are financially compensated for relocation and allocated a replacement flat that is brand new. This will certainly relieve the burden on taxpayers and the national budget in financing future SERS.

Conclusion

The notion that HDB flats are good assets and the pride we feel for high home-ownership rates may soon be things of the past. Back when Singapore was a landscape dotted with slums and squatters, the policies of asset enhancement through the ownership of homes were necessary and good. We have seen how Singapore's living condition improved by leaps and bounds to its current organised high-rise estates. However, having crossed 50 years of nation building, we now embark on a fresh new journey in a different era with different circumstances. Looking at the housing sector alone, we are already seeing new challenges.

From Chapter 1, you would have come to an understanding that the ageing population may result in an oversupply of resale flats in 15 years' time. That selling pressure will lead to a decline in housing prices and the decline will, unfortunately, be compounded with the depreciating 99-year leases.

The ageing population and decaying HDB leases are challenges that we are facing for the first time. Changes in lifestyle trends such as home-sharing will impact demand for residential properties. It is imperative that we consider changing our housing policies in anticipation of these challenges so that our future generations will live better than we do.

3. Concept Plan 2021:
What's Next for Singapore's Built Environment?

The article was co-authored with Muhammad Izzat Afiq Bin Othman, an undergraduate from the Department of Real Estate, National University of Singapore.

An Efficient, Pragmatic and Well-Planned Metropolis

Not many cities on Earth can rival Singapore's urban development in the past half a century. Clean, efficient and well-planned, the city's urban planning has been acknowledged as the hallmark of excellence and regarded as one of the best — if not the best — in the world.

In Singapore, land zoning is implemented strictly to ensure complementary land use; that the use of land in one area reinforces, and does not harmfully affect, the land use in the surrounding areas. For example, amenities and commercial land uses are placed close to residential areas to provide recreation and convenience to residents. In addition, utilities, public transport and a wide range of infrastructure are seamlessly integrated into every precinct, linking up homes, hospitals, offices, malls, places of worship, parks and sports facilities. But how did Singapore get here?

Urban Planning in Singapore

Firstly, the Ministry of National Development (MND) identifies key objectives for Singapore — such as building affordable homes, or developing of business parks to attract investment. Next, the Urban Redevelopment Authority (URA), in collaboration with other government agencies, formulates plans to achieve the objectives — the Concept Plan, the Master Plan, and other implementation plans.

The Concept Plan is a strategic land use and transportation plan that guides Singapore's development over the next 40–50 years. It focuses on how the current urban landscape can be adapted to keep pace with changing world trends and land use needs. Reviewed every 10 years, the next Concept Plan is due to be released in 2021.

In comparison, the Master Plan translates the broad, long-term strategies of the Concept Plan into detailed plans for implementation by specifying the permissible land uses and densities. It is a statutory land use plan which guides Singapore's development in the medium term over 10 to 15 years. Aside from the Concept and Master Plans, other implementation plans provide specific details on how land can be developed to meet the objectives highlighted in the Plans.

Trends to be Considered in Concept Plan 2021

In this article, we highlight several trends which will bring massive disruptions to the way we use real estate. Such trends include driverless vehicles, the rise of co-living, the increasing adoption of co-working spaces, the rise of FinTech and blockchain, the impact of climate change, and the innovation in education through EdTech. Concept Plan 2021 (CP2021) has to consider all these trends to ensure that Singapore's built environment is future-proofed. However, no prediction about the future trends can ever be certain. Even though these trends have to be taken into consideration for the CP2021, we have to incorporate sufficient flexibility to adapt to technological improvements and unforeseen circumstances.

The Advent of Driverless Vehicles

Once believed to be the stuff of science fiction and retrofuturism, it is now widely accepted that driverless vehicles could soon be widely adopted by the year 2025. Around the world, companies such as Tesla and Waymo are racing to develop these vehicles, and in Singapore, start-up nuTonomy is developing software to power the vehicles.

Rapid advancements in various fields such as artificial intelligence, motion sensors and radars have all contributed to the development of this technology. In fact, driverless vehicles could well be the greatest breakthrough in the automotive and transport industry since assembly lines. With driverless vehicles, drivers become commuters; and as they can spend their transit time more productively, the car becomes an extension of their office.

It is reasonable to assume that the arrival of driverless vehicles would impact parking spaces the most. Today, car owners like to park their vehicles close to their destination for convenience. But what if these vehicles can autonomously look for parking lots farther away?

In the near future, most vehicles will no longer need to be parked in buildings located in the prime locations within the Central Business District (CBD). Autonomous vehicles can let the car owners alight at their destinations, park elsewhere, and only return to pick up the owners when required. It is the same as calling for a taxi using the mobile apps today, except that the car of the future does not come with a driver.

As such, multi-storey car parks could be located at the fringe of the CBD where land costs are lower. As parking lots often cause congestions in areas of heavy traffic, it is likely that the shifting of parking spaces to outside of urban centres will reduce congestion. Even before driverless vehicles become the norm, CP2021 will need to include three elements in our urban plan; these are:

- to build wider drop-off points with shelter for all the buildings, especially those in the CBD,
- to have parking spaces relocated away from buildings in the CBD, and
- to allow existing car parks in buildings, where physically possible, to be converted into productive Gross Floor Area (GFA) or Lettable Area.

The above considerations could also apply to real estate segments such as retail, industrial and hotel, etc. What is important to note is that, say in the year 2035, when driverless cars are commonplace, there will be millions of square feet of car park space that could be repositioned as productive GFA. This means that we may be able to increase our total GFA by renovating existing buildings instead of building new ones.

Driverless vehicles also include delivery trucks and taxis. What happens when tens of thousands of drivers' jobs, say for commercial vehicles, is lost to technology? We guess that challenge has to be dealt with by the manpower plan.

Rise of Co-Living

Another trend which can alter our urban landscape in the foreseeable future is co-living. While it may be unheard of in Singapore, it has been surging in popularity overseas. Perhaps a good example would be Old Oak, a co-living space in London.

Co-living spaces emphasise community amongst neighbours. At its very core, co-living spaces are a hybrid of private and shared residential spaces. Tenants at co-living spaces will, of course, have their own private areas — such as bedrooms and kitchens — but more importantly, co-living spaces are designed to bring neighbours together. Co-living spaces have multiple communal areas within a building or a gated compound where neighbours can interact. For example, neighbours can go to the roof gardens to socialise, or head down to a lounge to play a game of foosball. Housekeeping services such as cleaning and laundry are also provided, bringing convenience to tenants. It is like housing an entire kampong within a residential block.

Co-living spaces could soon be adopted in Singapore as it serves several societal trends. Firstly, research has shown that a rising number of Singaporeans, young and old, are living alone.[1] Studies have shown that living alone for extended periods of time can lead to depression and possibly mental health issues. In co-living spaces, individuals can connect with others and be part of a wider community, akin to an extended family. This concept can also be applied to expatriates who live alone in Singapore.

Secondly, the concept of co-living can also be extended to old-age care. In Singapore, there has been an increase in the number of senior citizens living without their children. These senior citizens are not terminally ill and do not require 24-hour medical care. However, problems may arise for senior citizens during emergencies. A co-living space, with access to emergency assistance, can be a solution. Furthermore, the communal nature and "kampong spirit" promoted by co-living space can further enhance the sense of belonging for the elderly.

Singapore has a growing pool of senior citizens and that is an irreversible fact. Government projections have shown that one in four citizens will be over the age of 65 by the year 2050. Many of them will choose to sell their homes for cash and then move into a co-living space. The market sub-segment of co-living spaces which cater to able-bodied retirees are also called assisted living facilities.[2]

The trends pointing towards co-living spaces is all too clear. Co-living spaces can be built in the heartlands to ensure that prices remain affordable and within reach of ordinary Singaporeans. A possible option would be to recycle existing state properties, such as the dozens of disused schools, to become co-living spaces. This would probably require an inter-ministerial committee, such as the ministries of Community, National Development, Health and Education, to reposition the land use from schools to co-living residential use.

The upward trend of co-living will affect our existing public and private housing stock. We also need to take note that there will be selling pressure created by baby boomers who retire and

---

[1] Reference: http://www.straitstimes.com/singapore/more-singaporeans-living-alone-trend-seen-rising

[2] Reference: http://www.todayonline.com/singapore/elderly-dont-mind-assisted-living-facilities-survey

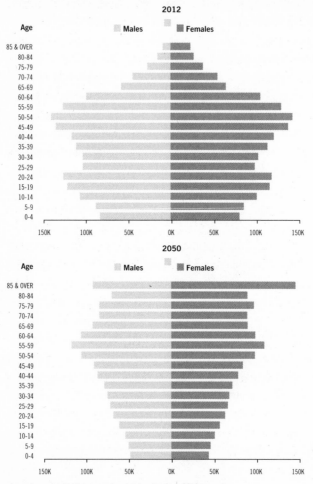

Figure 1: Singapore citizens' age profile in the year 2012, projected to the year 2050. Source: Population White Paper 2013

Assuming current birth rates and no immigration from 2013 onwards
Source: DOS

monetise their homes. Overall, we may need fewer new residential spaces to house the growth in population than we expect. CP2021 will need to taper down the policies governing future HDB sales and Government Land Sales so as to balance against the housing demand shifting from public and private housing towards co-living options. The monetization of homes for retirement needs simply adds more urgency to this point. Co-living spaces and a large dose of healthcare facilities have to feature strongly in CP2021.

Increase in Co-Working Spaces

We may be forgiven for not noticing this trend in Singapore, but co-working has already taken off in the major developed economies. In the last decade, the number of co-working spaces worldwide has increased tremendously. WeWork — a start-up which pioneered the development of co-working spaces in 2010 — now has more than 200 offices globally and had a market valuation of $20 billion in July 2017. The rise of WeWork has spawned various co-working space owners and operators, all of whom are trying to capitalise on this increasingly popular concept.

Co-working spaces are a form of shared working environment where its users come from different organizations. Typically, co-working spaces employ an open office model with individuals working around large desks so as to foster collaboration and knowledge sharing, sometimes in the hope of sparking off innovation. Co-working spaces have surged in popularity in the past few years due to a few reasons.

Firstly, office rentals have become exorbitantly expensive in many cities. Such high rents have deterred start-ups and businesses which are strapped for cash. Furthermore, businesses often face other hurdles such as rigid, long-term lease requirements and high renovation costs. Most office spaces are also under-utilised.

Secondly, the private sector is also leaning towards the formation of a global gig economy; jobs are temporary and flexible, and workers are independent contractors instead of being full-time employees. Through a laptop with internet access, workers can work in any locations convenient or comfortable to them, including during their commute inside driverless cars.

With these two reasons, it is easy to see why co-working spaces are becoming common: they are cheaper and more convenient alternatives to traditional offices. Unlike a traditional office, more than one company can share the premises, reducing rental costs and maximizing the use of available space. Furthermore, flexibility is built into the equation as workers can come and go as and when required, paying for the office premises only when they use it. This dovetails into the flexible nature of gig economy workers.

In the near future, co-working spaces are likely to be an integral part of Singapore's work environment. Companies such as Spacemob and The Hive have already opened co-working spaces. In July 2017, UrWork, a Chinese co-working space operator, launched its first overseas branch in Singapore's JTC LaunchPad @ one-north in an attempt to expand globally.

CP2021 needs to forecast how the rise of co-working spaces will impact our long held policies around the planning and supply of traditional office clusters. Demand for traditional offices is likely to fall as more gig economy companies opt for cheaper and more flexible co-working spaces. Furthermore, the sharing nature in a co-working environment optimises the use of space, increasing the number of workers per square foot of floor area.

In addition, co-working spaces may be planted in the HDB heartlands to accommodate the increase in gig economy workers, providing convenience for them to travel to work. Doing so would reduce congestion in populated business districts in Singapore's CBD and Jurong.

All the above trends in the office market, taken together with driverless cars that double up as "offices", means that we have to cast a critical eye on how we might expand the definition of commercial spaces over the next few decades.

Innovation in Education through EdTech

The proliferation of the internet in 1990s was truly phenomenal. Through the internet, information and ideas were able to spread quickly and transcend borders with a single click. In fact, similar to the discovery of the printing press in the 15th century, it can be argued that the internet, too, will transform the nature of education. Since its inception, the internet has been used as a medium to cater to long-distance learning and complement traditional learning methods. Students in Singapore have, for a while, been familiar with e-learning.

The current rise of Education Technology (EdTech) include: multi-modal learning that supplements classroom time with experiential learning and electronic means of delivering content, the recording of lectures which are uploaded online for students to revise at a later date, on-site learning supported by mobile devices, and e-assessments conducted outside schools. EdTech also encompasses new applications such as virtual classrooms, community learning tools, online assessments platforms, etc.

But how will EdTech impact a real estate concept plan?

With EdTech, a substantial number of learning hours can be remotely delivered. Students and adult learners may learn off-campus, at home, at their work sites, in a library or at a café. In the future, students will only need to attend school for hands-on sessions such as laboratory work, tutorial classes and practical assessments. In impoverished regions of emerging economies, the nearest schools are not only inconvenient to access, but poorly equipped. Here, EdTech provides opportunities for students to learn from their homes.

With a reduction in the number of physical hours in school, the utilisation of lecture halls and classrooms will drop. Depending on whether the subjects taught require laboratories and physical workshops, we can envisage that most institutions enabled with EdTech may double or triple their student intake without having to expand their physical premises.

Alternatively, where schools may be sitting on prime land, the size of the schools' premises can be reduced. Through clever scheduling of the academic calendar to balance the requirements for online and in-class learning, we may end up with having fewer classrooms yet increase the annual student enrolment.

What about the unused space in schools? As discussed above, the empty spaces in schools can be repurposed for co-living spaces. EdTech and the fast evolving teaching methods do not simply impact lecture halls and classrooms. We believe that schools which adopt EdTech extensively will reduce their need for student hostels too. This is particularly true for educational institutions that are leading the EdTech charge, particularly the top universities in Australia, the UK and the U.S. We caution investors to be doubly careful about investment opportunities in the student hostel segment in these countries.

Climate Change and Energy

As the world marches forward into the middle of the 21st century, sustainability has been a recurring theme. The rapid increase in world population, increasing urbanisation, and overconsumption of resources have led to climate change. The real estate industry has widely adopted the use of green technology. Some examples include PARKROYAL on Pickering, a hotel which leverages on green technology; CleanTech Park, Singapore's first eco-business park; and Gardens by the Bay, a garden at the heart of Marina Bay whose aim is to reduce urban heat waves. Plans for constructing sustainable housing estates, such as one for the upcoming eco-friendly Tengah "Forest Town", are greatly welcomed. However, such implementation may be insufficient for our next generation.

CP2021 must ensure that Singapore takes a big, bold step beyond these. More could be done to reduce carbon emissions and energy consumption in current buildings. Subsidies could be given to upgrading buildings, such as constructing 3D solar towers to reduce electricity consumption from non-renewable energy to shift to clean technology.[3]

CP2021 should take Singapore into energy independence by allocating space for solar, wind, tidal or other sustainable forms of energy production. Ample rooftop spaces across HDB towns can support an extensive solar grid, but given the numerous rainy and overcast days, we could supplement our electricity production with wind and tidal energy sources too.

Singapore has everything to lose if CP2021 fails to address the need for energy independence.

3D Printing and the Overhaul of Supply Chains

3D printing technology has started to take off, but widespread adoption may still be a decade or two away. However, it is not difficult to imagine how it will affect manufacturing, stock-keeping, logistics and supply chains processes.

Researchers from the S. Rajaratnam School of International Studies at Nanyang Technological University published a commentary earlier this year regarding how Asia's manufacturing economies might be disrupted by 3D printing.[4] They recounted that the assembly line, as pioneered by Henry Ford, required only low-skilled workers who could easily be taught simple, repetitive procedures. Mass production drove down unit costs of production, improved productivity, employment growth and put steady income into the hands of workers, many of whom used to be labourers and farmers.

However, 3D printing will replace mass production. Customisation and small-quantity production are possible, reducing the time-to-market for new products and allowing for many variations of a product to be produced in smaller batches. While mass production looks for cost efficiency by locating factories near to the source of raw material or the source of cheap labour, 3D printing companies will site themselves near to the points of consumption of their products. Labour and raw material costs are less important than the speed and variety of products that can be custom-made for the consumer. On this point, Singapore's small consumer market puts

---

[3] Reference: https://futurism.com/mit-building-3d-solar-towers-far-achieved-phenomenal-results/

[4] Reference: https://theconversation.com/how-3d-printing-could-disrupt-asias-manufacturing-economies-69633

it at a disadvantage in attracting 3D printing firms to be sited here.

The researchers wrote, "The direct implication of this is an extensive disruption in global supply chains, with jobs in manufacturing, logistics and warehousing being affected across many countries. Along with these, cargo transportation and port configuration would also be transformed due to the changes from economies of scale to the economy of one or few."

The commentary concluded that 3D printing will have major effects on China's and ASEAN's industrialisation and supply chain blueprints, and cautioned that transformation would be required beyond the manufacturing sector. In light of "potential upheavals", urban planning, land usage for manufacturing and warehousing, sea port and airport developments will need to be revamped.

Adding to the above, trade routes are altering due to China's Belt and Road Initiative. The overland route connects North Asia to Europe by rail in three weeks, half the time it takes for sea cargo to move via Singapore, the Straits of Malacca, India and the Middle East. This overland route also saves money and reduces risks for shippers who are moving goods between Europe and Asia.

If our planners took the above into consideration for CP2021, would they review the need to resize Tuas mega port and reallocate land and financial resources to other uses? Is the decades-old success formula of Singapore's hub-and-spoke economic model still relevant in the future, where point-to-point and peer-to-peer models are gaining momentum? Given the transformation of manufacturing, supply chains, logistics and warehousing, should CP2021 begin to redefine industrial land use in order to pave the way for an eventual merger with commercial land?

The Way Forward?

The truth is that there is no way to know what the future will be like. Trends discussed in this article may influence our urban landscape in many different ways, or they may die off or get superseded by other trends. We are at the start of the Fourth Industrial Revolution (or Industry 4.0) and technology is advancing at an unprecedented rate, such that new trends pop up every year.

Flying cars, once thought to be an element of Hollywood fantasy, are being tested. Singapore's Ministry of Transport is now in talks with companies making passenger drones to assess their viability.[5] It is a matter of time that drones can safely and economically ferry passengers, CP2021 will have to incorporate drone landing pads on and around buildings, as well as provide airspace for "roads".

We are stepping into uncertainty — the degree of which is probably a lot murkier than when plans for CP2011, or those before it, were drawn up.

What Else Should Be Considered in CP2021?

We have merely touched on a few obvious trends that require deeper consideration for Singapore's Concept Plan 2021. The trends discussed above encompass a fraction of all the emerging trends around the world.

There is one common thread between the three trends of co-working, co-living and EdTech: the world economy may grow but the demand for floor space will drop. The retail segment is a great example: e-commerce has reduced the demand for physical stores and malls, and many established shopping belts around the world are suffering from high vacancies.[6] Our retail icon Orchard Road is not spared.

In Japan, disruptions to traditional manufacturing and supply chains have, in some examples, led to the conversion of factories and warehouses to high-tech indoor farms which can produce vegetables around the clock. Our industrial land use policies will need to cater for obsolescence and irrelevance.

---

[5] Reference: http://www.dailymail.co.uk/sciencetech/article-4345244/Flying-TAXIS-hitting-Singapore-2030.html
[6] Reference: http://www.zerohedge.com/news/2017-03-07/third-all-shopping-malls-are-projected-close-space-available-signs-go-all-over-ameri

The Population White Paper 2013 was premised on a steady GDP growth that generates jobs, leading to an increase in immigration that will support population growth. Unfortunately, this premise may not hold true in Industry 4.0 as positive GDP growth could be achieved through high-value, high-productivity work that may, in fact, lead to job losses.

CP2021 has to consider a future economy where GDP growth will be achieved even as long-term resident unemployment increases and the need for workers shrink. This implies that fewer foreigners will need to be employed in Singapore, and the target of a 6.5–6.9 million population set out in White Paper 2013 may not be met. This will add further pressure to the risks of an oversupply in the residential market.

Another paper charting Singapore's economic blueprint is the 2017 report by the Committee on the Future Economy (CFE). Published in February 2017, the CFE Report proposed seven strategies for 23 industry sectors such as precision engineering, sea transport, financial services, etc. However, there was a glaring omission: the report did not note the irreversible trend of our ageing population and therefore, it did not address the increasing need for a deeper and wider range of healthcare services.

The CP2021 gives Singapore an opportunity to address the gaps in the Population White Paper 2013 and the CFE Report 2017.

And even as we look forward into the next 50 years with a concept plan, we must not forget to make plans for the older housing and industrial estates or commercial centres in Singapore. Most of the older precincts will require extensive makeovers in order to adapt to technological advances.

In sum, Concept Plan 2021 will have to anticipate future trends. It needs to shape Singapore's urban environment building with sufficient agility while also leaving enough flexibility to upgrade the Lion City so that it can remain relevant and grow.

4. Makeshift Patching Will Not Fix Defects in the Singapore Property Market

20 & 21 April 2016, Business Times

A series of cooling measures progressively introduced in the last six years has led to a patchwork quilt covering the property market, and that is now becoming uncomfortably scratchy and somewhat suffocating. Calls on the government to relax the cooling measures started two years ago, some predicting that measures will be relaxed in 2015. In the recent months, developers, property agents and industry associations, have repeated their calls with some predicting that measures may be lifted or amended by the end of 2016.

With recent Government Land Sales still seeing strong responses with eight to 10 bids per land tender, and with developers and property agents clocking in commendable profits for 2015, I do not think that cooling measures will be relaxed until such profits turn negative.

Since 2010, the cooling measures have added on to a list of "defects" in our property market that may culminate in a significant deterioration of property values over the next few decades. We examine six issues that will further widen the cracks in this article.

Firstly, the Executive Condominium (EC) segment provides a clear illustration of the extent of oversupply in the residential market. The term "sandwiched class" households implies a small market segment, sandwiched between the families that are eligible to buy new HDB flats and the wealthier families that can afford private properties. Since ECs were re-launched for sale in November 2010, and up till February 2016, developers have managed to satisfy the needs of 14,700 sandwiched households.

During that period, the household monthly income cap for EC buyers was raised from $10,000 to $12,000 in 2011 to widen the buyer pool. Amidst softening demand, the household income ceiling was further revised upwards to $14,000 per month in August 2015. Despite families with $14,000 per month of household income standing at the 77th percentile of households ranked by income levels, these families that can well afford ECs are further funded by generous subsidies from taxpayers. Yet sales of ECs continued to be lethargic.

The number of EC units launched but were left unsold climbed rapidly in the last year, allowing us to conclude that (1) we have already exhausted most of the demand for ECs and (2) raising the income ceiling did not lead to a significant additional demand. Added on the data point that as of 31 December 2015, there were 1,540 completed EC units that remained vacant (yes, vacant despite a Minimum Occupation Period rule), it means that even the category of "EC investors" have been exhausted.

Secondly, Singapore has relatively few economic policies and taxes that positively discriminate against foreigners and Permanent Residents (PRs). The Additional Buyer Stamp Duty (ABSD) is an exception. In addition to deterring foreigners and PRs from investing in Singapore's residential market, this policy has turned Singapore's desire to be a wealth planning hub on its head. Wealthy families that have invested heavily in Singapore and that are now considering estate and succession planning find their options limited when it comes to their residential assets. Before ABSD was introduced, these families could transfer their properties into a living trust or a foundation by paying the normal stamp duty of just under 3%. With the ABSD of 15%, transferring your accumulated residential assets

Figure 1: Total number of EC units launched but unsold on a monthly basis

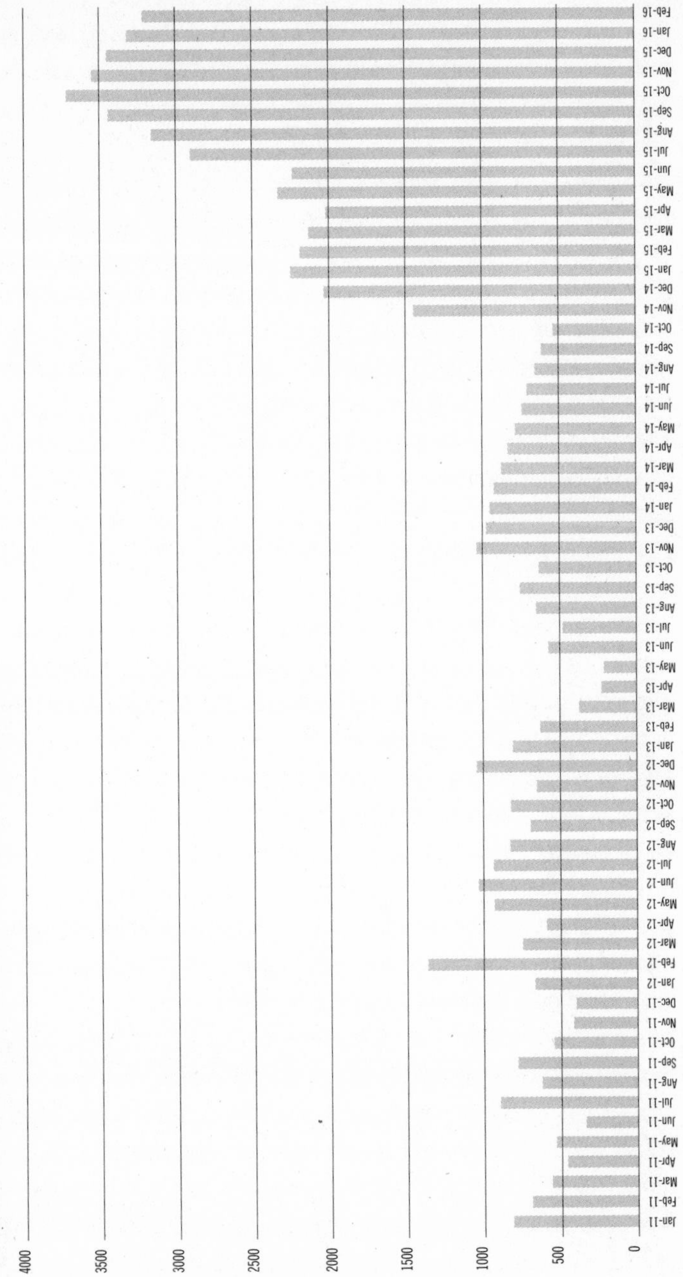

Source: URA, Century 21 (IPA)

to a trust will cost a prohibitive 18% in duties. So ABSD does not just cool the residential market, it also cooled the wealth planning industry, slowing down the business for trust managers, bankers and lawyers.

Thirdly, the most successful measure that curbed excessive residential investments termed the Total Debt Servicing Ratio (TDSR), has discounted the value of real estate assets to almost zero. Introduced in mid-2013, TDSR defines the maximum loan for residential properties based on the ability of the borrower to repay the monthly mortgage, stress-tested at 3.5% per annum interest rates for residential properties and 4.5% for commercial properties. The TDSR framework regards a borrower's income and type of income (e.g. commissions, fixed salary, dividends, ad hoc fees, etc.) as the main source of mortgage repayment and the loan size and loan tenure are determined based on the borrower's age and credit worthiness.

The globally accepted practice of asset-backed lending for real estate does not apply in Singapore once TDSR was implemented. Since the income of the borrower is the main determinant of the size of the property loan, the value of the property itself is secondary. This inherently means that a retiree of age 65 without income and living in a fully paid private apartment that is worth $500,000, or $5 million, or S$50 million for that matter, will not be able to take a dollar of loan against the property to sustain his daily cashflow needs. Where is the inherent value of this piece of real estate called home if in the eyes of the banks and the authorities, value only exists in the income of the borrower?

The fourth issue is a misguided method of controlling prices through massive land supply. Our policy planners adopt the method of capping prices in the residential market by ensuring that a sufficiently large pipeline of supply is available to home buyers and developers. The rationale is that increasing the sales of new HDB flats and private residences will lead to more competition amongst sellers and keep a lid on price growth. The exuberant pace of sales since Singapore pulled out of the Global Financial Crisis in 2009 has led to a massive boom in construction. Between 2011 to 2015, the total stock of Singapore's residential units, net of demolitions, increased by about 150,000 and between 2016 to 2019, another 155,000 residential units will be completed.

While the Building & Construction Authority has reported better performance and higher scores in construction quality across both HDB flats, ECs and private residential projects, there are also more and more high profile cases of building defects, some of which have resulted in lawsuits. Cases of building defects in new developments highlighted by the media included million dollar homes such as The Sea View, RiverParc Residence, The Sail @ Marina Bay and The Coast in Sentosa Cove.

Given the large number of properties being built, these cases may be regarded as negligible when compared to the number of homes that are properly built. However, what might negatively impact future home values is a recent landmark ruling by the High Court. Owners of The Sea View who sued for numerous alleged defects were told by the High Court that the developer, the architect and the main contractor are largely not liable for negligence claims because most of the work had been delegated to other companies, or independent contractors.

One implication for all Singapore property investors might be: investors would need to know the whole plethora of contractors engaged by the developer, the architect or the main contractor for any work on the property. Should investors find any defects in the property and their claims against the developer, the architect and the main contractor did not result in any compensation, the investors would have to direct their claims further down the food chain, directly at the company that had specifically performed the work resulting in the defects.

Such a ruling incentivises developers and main contractors to outsource more of their work. Coupled with the increasing incidences of shoddy workmanship and building defects, the finished quality of real estate might drop, as would its value.

The fifth flaw relates to the slowly but increasingly complex set of rules around Singapore property investments. In addition to the various layers of buyer and seller stamp duties, property taxes are tiered and strata area laws are perplexing even to seasoned real estate professionals. An investor purchasing 2,000 sqft of strata area could have as little as 1,200 sqft of usable floor area: a drop of about 40%. The large difference between the area we paid for and the area we can use lies mainly in the void. Yes, the airspace between us and the ceiling, if the ceiling is above certain height limits in a residential or a non-residential space, termed "internal void", is considered "sellable strata area". Stretching our imagination further, in strata landed houses, investors pay for several levels of "external void" strata area between themselves and the sky.

Strata void areas proliferated in the last decade and extended themselves into office and industrial segments. The investors paid for the void which is of little interest to tenants, especially in the industrial category where the size of the production floor area is a key determinant of rental discussions.

As our economy progresses with technological changes, the rules around various category of industrial uses are also getting muddled and, in most circumstances, require more precise definitions. Overall, hazy rules coupled with complicated duties and taxes will make our properties less and less attractive to serious, long-term investors.

The final point: our housing policy. It served us superbly well in the nation-building years of Singapore. Looking forward, it is more likely to be a millstone around our necks in a future economy which has shorter boom-bust cycles and which is more nimble.

Chapter 1 in my book *Weathering a Property Downturn* discusses the merits of Singapore's drive for high home-ownership rates during its formative years, and the first five decades of nation-building has its merits. But this "achievement" did not come without its sacrifices.

At just over 90%, Singapore's home ownership rate is very high compared to developed nations such as 36% for Switzerland (one of the role-model countries for Singapore), 45% for Germany, 64% for the UK, 64% for the USA, 61% for Japan and 67% for Australia. These are countries which consistently generate more innovative, world-leading products than Singapore.

Figure 2: Singapore ranks third in this chart comparing owner-occupier rates for homes across 35 countries. But is it a good thing?

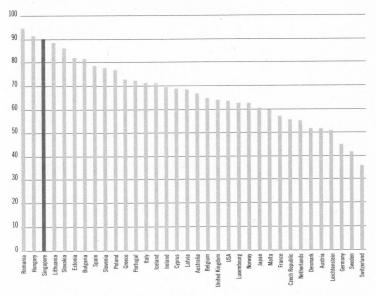

Source: Century 21 (International Property Advisor Pte Ltd); Eurostat, People in the EU: Who we are and how do we live 2015 edition; Australian Bureau of Statistics (from population census 2011); Statistical Survey Department, Statistics Bureau, Ministry of Internal Affairs and Communications, Japan (from population census 2013); SingStat (2014)

As Singapore seeks to transform its workforce to be more innovative, entrepreneurial and nimble-footed, we need to adapt our housing policy to the needs of a future global economy that rewards asset-light, agile and adaptive entrepreneurs. Handcuffing our young households with 30-year-long mortgages when they get married at 28 years of age will not foster any entrepreneurial spirit.

In fact it does the opposite, making our society of well-educated workers averse to risk, and happy to just conform to the status quo. A housing policy that encourages high home ownership may put a drag on future economic growth. And eventually a reduction in the value of its real estate.

The six "defects" are similar to the cracks in a leaking roof. We could keep patching the six cracks as they slowly split wider. And we could patch new cracks as they appear, such as through game-changing trends like short term home-sharing. But even if the roof does not buckle and give way, continuous patching of cracks will bring down home values.

5. Singaporeans Are Ageing Fast: Let's Get Planning

10 June 2016, TODAY

I am not bringing up this subject because I see my hairline receding rapidly or because I need bifocals. If we took a snapshot of Singapore's population tree in 2015 and assumed that the population was with us all the while (i.e. no inward nor outward migration) 400,000 residents celebrated their 60th birthdays between 2006 and 2015, and in the next 10 year period between 2016 and 2025, more than 600,000 residents will celebrate their 60th year on earth.

Our resident population in 2015 was 3.9 million, of which 700,000 or 18% were already over 60 years of age. If we froze the population based on the 2015 demographics, and accounting for about 19,000 residents who pass away every year, by the year 2025, at least 30% of us will be over 60 years old. That equates to over 1.1 million Singapore residents.

I am not qualified to discuss concerns about the "old-age support ratio" that is dropping fast, nor the issues we face when fewer and fewer residents contribute to CPF while more and more will draw down on their CPF accounts. I am concerned about whether our Master Plan has catered for sufficient land for healthcare facilities to soothe my aching bones when I am older.

Need to Expand Hospital Capacity

Our current estimated capacity is 2.3 hospital beds per 1,000 population. While some may deem this ratio adequate for Singapore's needs, I doubt it is sufficient in the next 10 years.

Firstly, as a population ages, the demand for beds will increase even if our total population remained constant. Secondly, our situation was made worse as the big 1.1 million jump in Singapore's population in the last 10 years was not matched by a corresponding increase in the number of hospital beds. Thirdly, our international promotion for medical tourism since 2003 meant that the 2.3 beds per 1,000 population are shared with foreign visitors.

Figure 1: Singapore's total population versus the number of beds in private and public hospitals

Year	Singapore's total population	Total number of hospital beds	Hospital beds per 1,000 population
2006	4,401,400	10,358	2.4
2007	4,588,600	10,406	2.3
2008	4,839,400	10,312	2.1
2009	4,987,600	10,387	2.1
2010	5,076,700	10,283	2.0
2011	5,183,700	10,334	2.0
2012	5,312,400	10,755	2.0
2013	5,399,200	10,969	2.0
2014	5,469,700	11,230	2.1
2015	5,535,000	12,903*	2.3*

* Assuming that all 700 beds in Ng Teng Fong General Hospital, 400 beds in Jurong Community Hospital, 428 beds in Yishun Community Hospital and 145 beds in Farrer Park Hospital were fully operational in 2015 and that no existing beds were decommissioned.

Source: SingStat, Ministry of Health, Singapore, Farrer Park Hospital, Jurong Health, Century 21 (IPA)

We have received accolades as a world-class healthcare hub over the years. However, we are far behind the world's best in several key metrics. For example, Monaco and Japan lead the world with 16.0 and 13.4 beds per 1,000 population respectively.

And while having 2.3 physicians per 1,000 population might seem high as compared to our neighbours, the World Health Organization ranked Singapore 71st for this measure.

Naysayers

Many well-educated members of the elite are in fact opposed to the idea that we should expand our hospital capacity to rise to a level closer to other developed nations such as Australia or Switzerland. They point to the fact that Singaporeans are eating and living healthier in a clean and hygienic environment, therefore we do not require as many hospital beds.

Others offer the counter-intuitive argument that the more hospital capacity we build, the more demand will surface as patients will opt to stay longer in the hospitals when more beds are available. On this matter, I find it difficult to imagine anyone wanting to stay in a hospital beyond what is required, as staying in hospitals can by no means be considered recreational.

New Developments

In the past few years, plans for several new precincts were announced: Woodlands Regional Centre, Jurong Lake District, Paya Lebar Central, Marina South Residential District, Bidadari, Tampines North and Punggol Matilda. In scrutinising each of these areas, I look for land parcels earmarked for healthcare, such as for polyclinics and hospitals.

The 1,400-bed Sengkang General and Community Hospitals and the 550-bed Outram Community Hospital are currently under construction. The total number of polyclinics across the island, which remained at 18 for more than a decade, is expected to increase to 20 by the year 2017 with new polyclinics in Pioneer and Punggol and then rise to 22 by the year 2020 when Bukit Batok Polyclinic and another primary healthcare facility open in Sembawang/Admiralty.

Unfortunately, I am not able to find land allocated for additional healthcare facilities beyond the year 2020 in especially in the new precincts of Bidadari and Tampines North, which are expected to add tens of thousands of homes.

Recommendations

In view of the expected rapid increase in the number of senior citizens, I wish that healthcare and our ageing population take top priority when our planners develop Master Plan 2019 (which guides Singapore's development over the medium term of about 10–15 years) and review the Concept Plan (which guides Singapore's development over 40–50 years).

The new land use plan could include building one new 500-bed public or private hospital per year between 2021 and 2030. This will bring a total of about 20,000 beds to serve the needs of a bigger but older population of 6.9 million population, or a ratio of 2.9 beds per 1,000 population in 2030. Still far from world class, but certainly an improvement from today.

Without forgetting the software, I suggest that we quickly build a new healthcare school to produce the full range of healthcare workers: nursing, doctors, physiologists, speech therapists, radiologists, pharmacists, caregivers for the terminally ill, facility managers, etc and with the added focus on geriatrics.

By doing so, we raise the quality of healthcare services for Singapore's population and we generate thousands of high-skilled, high-value workers for our economy. The healthcare school and the additional ten 500-bed hospitals will generate over 100,000 direct and indirect jobs.

There will also be positive spin-offs into areas such as medical research, diagnostics and healthcare products. In 20 years, healthcare might become a top contributor to the economic growth of Singapore even as our ageing population enjoy the convenience of expanded hospital capacities staffed by more and better-trained caregivers.

Author's Note

It seems odd that the issues of the ageing population and the increasing demands for healthcare services were not addressed in the "Report of the Committee on the Future Economy" published in February 2017. The Healthcare 2020 Masterplan was unveiled five years ago in 2012. I look forward to a comprehensive healthcare master plan that will specifically address new technological advances and the wide range of needs for training more healthcare workers, doctors, therapists and counsellors.

6. Recycling Tanglin Halt

The article was co-authored with Lee Sing Ying, an undergraduate from the Department of Real Estate, National University of Singapore.

Queenstown being Singapore's first satellite new town holds significant value to not only residents, but also to Singaporeans at large, especially the pioneer generation.

From squatter housing to a well-planned township, Queenstown has come a long way. The "chap lau chu" or 10-storey blocks of flats and the three-storey Singapore Improvement Trust (SIT) flats are significant architectural reminders that could be preserved for future generations to appreciate Singapore's early affordable-housing landscape.

In June 2014, the authorities announced that Tanglin Halt estate was identified for the Selective En bloc Redevelopment Scheme (SERS) and 31 blocks of flats will be vacated. Within these blocks of flats are clusters of amenities, including shophouses and markets.

With SERS, we relegate yet another part of our shared history and physical space to images, bytes and memories. Yet unlike most of the other 80 SERS projects, Tanglin Halt estate has a little bit of — pardon my French — *je ne sais quoi* about it.

There is a reason behind every SERS project. In the Master Plan for Queenstown, the government intends to create a self-sufficient town by ensuring that employment centres are present within the

Queenstown Planning Area with new housing choices available for working families who wish to live near to their workplaces.[1]

Lined up neatly like two rows of dominoes, the historic "chap lau chu" will be demolished when the residents have moved out after their replacement flats in Dawson and Forfar are ready from around 2020. In their place, Tanglin Halt could be filled with condominiums and new HDB flats. As early as the year 2030, the energy and vibe of Tanglin Halt could be transformed from an elderly-populated, laid back and peaceful neighbourhood to a younger and more energetic precinct.

The Case for Conserving Parts of Tanglin Halt

We are somewhat ambivalent about seeing the old blocks of flats demolished and redeveloped into new and tall HDB blocks, with modern designs, improved build-quality and better accessibility. We are motivated to appeal to concerned residents and the planning authorities to conserve several buildings and community spaces between these buildings. These spaces must have hosted countless memorable events for families in the past five to six decades since the birth of Tanglin Halt estate.

The most iconic feature would be the Tanglin Halt Community Plaza which is an open piazza, like a market square. This space, demarcated by three blocks of two-storey shophouses (Blocks 46-1, 46-2, 46-3) and the iconic tri-hexagon Commonwealth Drive Food Centre (Blocks 1A, 2A, 3A) should be conserved. Such traditional European market square layout is uncommon in Singapore today, but was a flavour in several of Singapore's early HDB estates.

Now, it would be meaningless if we proposed that the buildings around the open piazza be conserved without suggesting how they might be repositioned for future users.

---

[1] Source: URA Draft Master Plan 2013 for Queenstown Planning Area. https://www.ura.gov.sg/MS/DMP2013/regional-highlights/~/media/dmp2013/Planning%20Area%20Brochures/Brochure_Queenstown.ashx

The demolition of 31 blocks of flats, which contains about 3,800 housing units, could result in this entire neighbourhood being redeveloped into homes for more than 10,000 households in HDB flats and private condominiums. The new residential cluster would require a centralised commercial area where residents can go to for amenities and services.

We further suggest that in addition to this cluster of buildings around the Tanglin Halt Community Plaza, the adjacent cluster of buildings consisting of another three blocks of two-storey shophouses (Blocks 47, 48, 49) surrounding the Tanglin Halt Market (Block 48A) to be conserved. The buildings should be renovated and repositioned as the future commercial and neighbourhood centre of Tanglin Halt.

Figure 1: Map of Tanglin Halt

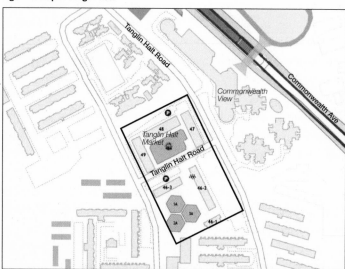

The blocks and spaces between the blocks (highlighted in the box) should be conserved and meaningfully re-positioned for use as a neighbourhood and commercial centre for the rejuvenated Tanglin Halt estate.

There are several reasons why we are proposing to conserve this "town square":

1. Love Mother Earth

As a responsible nation of the global community, it is good to be green and environmentally friendly. What is the point of giving out green building awards to various organizations when, all across Singapore, we keep tearing down buildings that could be repositioned?

2. We will need a commercial centre anyway

There will be more residents moving in than the existing ones who have been relocated due to SERS. These new residents will have a relatively younger demographic profile. In order to serve these new families, a commercial centre with a wider range of amenities will be needed.

This location is 100m from the Commonwealth MRT Station. Residents heading home or leaving home to the bus stop and MRT station can conveniently pass through this town square, run their errands, have their meals, pick up their children, etc.

We will require more facilities for infants and children than we do today. These include commercial spaces that can house day care centres, tuition centres, student enrichment companies, as well as offices for service providers such as maid agencies, etc. Space may also be allocated for municipal services, such as a town council office, police and civil defence posts.

This commercial centre may also provide job opportunities for some of the new residents.

3. Jobs may be housed here too

The Master Plan indicated self-sufficiency as an objective for Queenstown. Tanglin Halt used to be separated from the one-north and Bouna Vista area by a railway track, but that has been removed two years ago.

Now that the railway track is no more a barrier, Tanglin Halt's proximity to innovation centres such as the JTC LaunchPad at one-north and Biopolis at Buona Vista could allow it to play a support role to the innovation and technology businesses. A low density office precinct could be incorporated by refurbishing the two-storey shophouses around the town square in Tanglin Halt. These could be offices for incubators for tech start-ups, offices of venture capital providers, professional and legal services firms that support the tech start-ups and research organisations.

Bearing in mind that Tanglin Halt is located between the commercial hubs of Raffles Place CBD and the Jurong Lake District, we might develop the "Tanglin Halt-one-north-Bouna Vista" cluster to complement the needs of multinational companies. Hence the conserved buildings can be converted to boutique offices and co-working spaces to nurture a new hive of start-ups and encourage entrepreneurs to plant their flags here.

4. A social spot

But let us not forget the software: the Tanglin Halt Community Plaza is an open-air piazza that can host traditional cultural performances, pasar malams, street festivals, arts and craft displays, etc. It will be a place for families to celebrate events and occasions together under the stars.

This piazza will be a focal point for the whole neighbourhood, where residents gather for a relaxing evening and shoot the breeze as the world rolls by. The main draw will would be the ambience: a mix of 1960s buildings and the youthful energy of the new residents and workers.

Conclusion

We understand the government's initiative to rejuvenate the town for it to realise its potential. However, most times, our relentless pursuit for every square inch of real estate to be maximised to its best and highest value can leave us poorer as a nation, for we have demolished our shared memories. Why demolish the buildings around the piazza, and consequently lose the town square, when they can all be conserved and repositioned for better use?

PART 2

OBSERVATIONS ON THE RESIDENTIAL MARKET

7. Market Watchers Expecting Slashed Prices Will Be Waiting for Godot

4 March 2016, TODAY

Many calls have been made for the relaxation of property cooling measures since early 2015. Many market players also speculated about the reduction of the Additional Buyer Stamp Duty (ABSD) for residential properties last year, and since 2015 has passed, they have renewed their predictions that ABSD may be reduced in 2016.

Perceptive market watchers and property agents have gone one step further. They are guessing at which projects, faced with hefty penalties when the deadlines on the Qualifying Certificate (QC) and Additional Buyer Stamp Duty (ABSD) pass, would slash prices significantly to sell out and avoid the charges.

Any developers with foreign shareholders or directors must apply for a QC when they buy and develop private residential properties. Under the QC, they have to obtain the Temporary Occupation Permit (TOP) within five years and sell all the units within two years of TOP. Otherwise, there is an extension charge of 8%, 16% or 24% payable on the land cost in the first, second or third and subsequent years respectively, pro-rated based on the percentage of unsold apartments.

Developers who purchased land between 8 December 2011 and 11 January 2013 will be subject to the ABSD of 10%. Land purchased on or after 12 January 2013 will be subject to 15% ABSD. However, remission of five years is allowed for the sale of all the apartments. If there is even one unit left unsold at the end of the five-year deadline, the ABSD plus a 5% per annum interest charge on the land cost has to be paid to the authorities.

More than 40 projects across the island are exposed to QC and/ or ABSD charges in 2016 and 2017 if they do not sell out by their respective deadlines. Examples mentioned by analysts and the media include The Trilinq, The Crest, d'Leedon, The Creek @ Bukit, The Glades, etc.

Prospective investors are circling around projects with large numbers of unsold units, waiting to pounce on the developers who are pressured to reduce selling prices to avoid the penalties.

But will developers really slash prices?

Let us consider a simple example of ABSD charges for The Trilinq.

Project name	The Trilinq
Date of land sale	12 January 2012
Land price	$408,000,800.00
Deadline for ABSD remission	11 January 2017
Total number of units	755
Unsold units (as of Jan2016)	528
ABSD payable with 5% per annum interest	$52,072,390

Assuming that sales efforts are stepped up and an average of 30 apartments are sold each month for the next 11 months such that by January 2017, there would be 200 units left. The market price of the remaining 200 units, at an average price of $1.3 million each, could total $260 million.

The developer has two choices. They could choose to pay the $52.1 million in ABSD with interest and continue to market the 200 unsold units.

Alternatively, the developer could choose to set up an investment holding company and buy over all the remaining 200 units, with no discount, at $260 million. They then foot the Normal Stamp Duty of $6.61 million and a 15% ABSD of $39 million, i.e. a total stamp duty expense of $45.61 million. This alternative is lower in cost, the project is considered "sold out" and the developer can lease out the units to generate income as soon as construction is completed.

Moreover, if the market watchers got their wishes fulfilled and the authorities did reduce ABSD by the end of 2016, the total stamp duty bill would be even lower than $45.6 million.

The advantages do not end there. This alternative will allow the developer to avoid slashing prices in order to achieve a complete sell-out, such that valuations of the project and other private residences in its vicinity will not be impacted. The last thing developers would want is to spark off a price war amongst themselves and other urgent sellers in the resale market.

The market is rife with speculations about the lifting of property cooling measures. Investors, financial analysts and property agents are also guessing which developers will blink in the face of ABSD and QC charges.

It does not help that neither the authorities nor industry associations publish any official data on the unsold units held by the developers. To complicate matters, shortly after the projects receive their TOP and the Certificate of Statutory Completion (CSC), they fall out of the purview of the Controller of Housing, further limiting the public data on the number of unsold units held by developers.

Let me reveal the plot: Godot does not turn up. If ABSD were relaxed, most developers and resale property owners will raise prices a little, offsetting part of the savings that buyers might gain. And looking at the list of 40 projects facing QC and ABSD charges in 2016 and 2017, I doubt that any developer will discount prices by more than 10% in order to achieve a faster pace of sales. Not unless extenuating conditions force them to.

8. The Case of Disappearing Households

13 May 2016, TODAY

Certain odd numbers around the residential markets have puzzled me lately. Let us consider two of these perplexing cases.

Firstly, while we get lots of news about the high rates of e-applications for Executive Condominiums (ECs), the queue numbers dished out did not translate into many apartments sold. Secondly, despite a slowing population growth and low foreigner employment growth, the increase in the number of occupied residential units has far exceeded the number of new households.

Puzzle 1: Phantom Applicants in New EC Launches

The process of launching an EC begins with a few weeks of product preview and getting prospective buyers to submit applications online. Before the booking day, developers and property agents would help buyers submit their e-applications, diligently checking submissions to ensure that the applicants meet all the eligibility conditions.

It is common to see developers and property agents engage the mainstream and social media to keep the public updated on the number of e-applications received. The market is kept excited about the increasing demand prior to the first day of sales, also known as the booking day.

For the 10 projects launched since January 2015, a total of 5,544 units available for sale attracted more than 5,993 e-applications, a very healthy over-subscription rate of 10%. However, in the first weekend that the ECs were open for booking, only 24% of the launched units were sold!

Figure 1: Since January 2015, the number of e-applicants for new EC launches is almost five times the number of units contracted during the launch weekends. Where did the applications — close to 4,700 of them — disappear to?

Project name	Launch date	Units launched	e-applications received	Units sold in the first weekend	Shortfall between e-applications received and units sold
The Amore Westwood	Jan-15	378	> 300	75	> 225
Residences	May-15	480	500	118	382
The Brownstone	Jul-15	638	640	185	455
The Vales	Jul-15	517	439	79	360
Sol Acres	Aug-15	707	800	248	552
Signature at Yishun	Sep-15	525	507	93	414
The Criterion	Oct-15	505	465	41	424
Wandervale	Mar-16	534	783	262	521
Visionaire	Apr-16	632	859	158	701
Parc Life	Apr-16	628	> 700	51	> 649
	Total	5544	> 5993	1310	> 4683

Note: Shaded area refers to projects launched after the annual household income ceiling was raised from $144,000 to $168,000.

Source: Century 21 (IPA), "EC e-applications not translating to sales" – Business Times, 6 May 2016

What happened to the 84% (or 4,683) of the applicants who backed out? Some of the applicants have taken the extra trouble to verify their eligibility, consult with their bankers and submit documents such as proof of income and marriage certificates.

How many are repeat applicants who submitted applications across several projects? What motivated them to do so?

What about the buyers who rushed to commit on the booking day? Did their sense of urgency turn into disappointment after they realised that the high e-application numbers did not translate into many sales?

I guess the agents and developers of each project are just as befuddled about who these phantom applicants are. Perhaps we will not get any answers unless we are able to analyse all the applications submitted for all these 10 projects.

Puzzle 2: Who Are Living in These Residences?

In the 12-month period ending in June 2013, Singapore had a population growth of 86,800 people, including foreign domestic workers (who do not need an additional housing unit). That same period saw an increase in 22,500 households in Singapore, including singles who might want to be independent from their families, young couples moving into new HDB flats, ECs and private residences. Newly married couples who continue to stay with their parents also add to the household count.

Figure 2: Comparing the increases in population and households with the increases in take up of HDB flats, ECs and private residences

	Population increase (including foreign domestic workers)	Increase in number of households	Increase in number of occupied HDB flats*	Increase in number of occupied EC units ^	Increase in number of occupied private residential units ^	Total increase in HDB, EC and private residential units
4 quarters till end June 2013	86,800	22,500	7,887	7	9,760	17,654
4 quarters till end June 2014	70,500	25,500	16,142	1,420	10,035	27,597
4 quarters till end June 2015	65,300	25,300	27,985	2,699	16,723	47,407
3 quarters till end March 2016	n.a.	n.a.	n.a.	2,937	11,931	n.a.

* The total number of HDB flats is based on end March of that reference year.
^ Occupied units derived from total stock minus vacant units.

Source: HDB, URA, SingStat, Century 21 (IPA)

The increases in population and households were accommodated by an additional 17,654 dwelling units, which included 7,887 HDB flats and an increased take up of 9,760 ECs and private residences.

For 2013, the increase in the number of occupied units seems reasonable when viewed against the population and household growth, since we have yet to account for the full range of accommodation types, such as student hostels, dormitories and serviced apartments. Fluctuations in vacancies are also not accounted for and I have further assumed that almost all new additions to the stock of HDB flats are occupied, as new HDB flats fall under the five-year Minimum Occupation Period (MOP).

The number of dwelling units occupied jumped by 27,597 in 2014, even as population growth slowed to 70,500 people and the number of resident households increased by 25,500.

A bigger jump happened in 2015. The population increased by a smaller number of 65,300 people (including about 9,000 foreign domestic workers) and the number of households grew by 25,300. However, these increases were accommodated by an additional 27,985 HDB flats and close to 20,000 more occupied ECs and private residences.

Did we really need an additional 47,407 dwelling units to accommodate a population growth of 65,300 and a household growth of 25,300? Pent-up demand from splitting family nucleus to spawn new households is already being accounted for here. Where did these occupiers come from?

As a property agent helping landlords to secure tenants for their investment apartments, it seems to me that the number of vacant residences is rising rapidly, which is why the competition for tenants is very stiff and rentals are dropping.

Furthermore, as reported by the Ministry of Manpower, more foreigners are losing their jobs and leaving Singapore. Given the weak jobs growth, the tight foreign worker policies and a new focus on restructuring our economy into a "labour-lean" workforce, the proportion of new housing supply seems to outstrip the potential demand from tenants. However, over the three quarters from 3Q2015 to 1Q2016, an additional 14,868 ECs and private residences were occupied.

Therefore, while having more than 4,683 missing EC applicants may seem odd, the big increase in the number of occupied residences seems bizarre, especially when viewed against a backdrop of weaker population and jobs growth.

9. No Lack of Space for 10 Million Population

16 May 2016, The Edge Property

> *"In land-scarce Singapore, investing in the right property can provide you with handsome returns."* — 99.co, 3 September 2015

> *"Land scarcity is a very real problem for Singapore which explains the ever-increasing land costs and property prices which are driven by pent up demand."* — SGPropertyReviews.com, 11 January 2014

Singaporeans have been brought up to accept such statements as a gospel truth. Many do not even question the meaning of scarcity and do not realise that Singapore's land size has increased by 100 square kilometres (sqkm) in the last 35 years. Add to that the advances in space planning, improved transport systems, enhanced construction capabilities leading to a much higher population density, and *voilà*, we have 5.54 million people today.

The brief statistics are, in the 35-year period between 1980 and 2015, our population grew by 129% from 2.41 million to 5.54 million, made possible by a 16% increase in land size from 617.9 sqkm to 719.1 sqkm and a 97% increase in population density from 3,907 people per sqkm to 7,697 people per sqkm. (See Figure 1)

Even though land reclamation has allowed us to increase our land mass, there are many amongst us who do not feel that there is ever enough, and continue to insist that 719.1 sqkm of land is considered scarce.

Scarce or otherwise, let us at least recognise that we have carried a misconception for several generations: the phrase "land is scarce" does not equate to "space is scarce". We have been stacking more and more people on top of one another and packing people closer together to create higher and higher population density. Look at the abundance of shoebox residential units!

Technology has improved. Our capabilities have improved. Lifestyles have changed. Today we are better able to accommodate higher population densities because of better construction standards, better space planning, better transport systems and we have flexible working hours with many knowledge workers working longer hours in cafés and from homes.

For those who have not been following developments of the Master Plan, we present a summary of various pieces of "work in progress" in the real estate front that will allow Singapore to accommodate a 10 million population from around the year 2050. We also make the bold assumption that the Transport and Health authorities are expanding their capacities to match the population increase.

Here is one more somewhat audacious assumption on the back of our low birth rates: Singapore's environments and economy will remain sufficiently attractive such that there is a constant stream of population inflow to sustain a population growth to 10 million people.

The following sections are based on scattered bits of public information announced over the past few years, which have been glued together with our assumptions. They will reveal to us how the residential landscape can evolve to house Singapore's growing population.

Existing HDB Towns — 535,144 More Units in the Pipeline

Figure 2 provides us with a glimpse of the long term dwelling plans undertaken by the Housing & Development Board (HDB). For 23 of the HDB towns, their total land area and the total number of flats currently being managed by HDB. The projected maximum number of dwelling units, which includes HDB flats and future government

Figure 1: Singapore's land size grew by 100 sqkm while her population grew by 3.1 million over the 35-year period from 1980 to 2015.

Year	Population	Land size	Population density (per sqkm)
1980[1]	2,413,945	617.9	3,907
1981	2,532,835	617.9	4,099
1982	2,646,466	618.0	4,282
1983	2,681,061	618.0	4,338
1984	2,732,221	620.3	4,405
1985	2,735,957	620.5	4,409
1986	2,733,373	621.6	4,397
1987	2,774,789	622.6	4,457
1988	2,846,108	625.7	4,549
1989	2,930,901	626.4	4,679
1990[1]	3,047,132	633.0	4,814
1991	3,135,083	639.2	4,905
1992	3,230,698	641.0	5,040
1993	3,313,471	641.4	5,166
1994	3,419,048	646.1	5,292
1995	3,524,506	647.5	5,443
1996	3,670,704	647.5	5,669
1997	3,796,038	647.8	5,860
1998	3,927,213	648.1	6,060
1999	3,958,723	659.9	5,999
2000[1]	4,027,887	682.7	5,900
2001	4,138,012	682.3	6,065
2002	4,175,950	687.1	6,078
2003	4,114,826	692.8	5,939
2004	4,166,664	696.0	5,987
2005	4,265,762	696.9	6,121
2006	4,401,365	698.9	6,298
2007	4,588,599	700.3	6,552
2008	4,839,396	706.9	6,846
2009	4,987,573	710.0	7,025
2010[1]	5,076,732	710.4	7,146
2011	5,183,688	712.7	7,273
2012	5,312,437	715.1	7,429
2013	5,399,162	716.1	7,540
2014	5,469,724	718.3	7,615
2015	5,535,002	719.1	7,697

Figure 1 Notes:

[1] Census of population

Prior to 2003, data are based on Singapore's land area as at end-December. From 2003 onwards, data are based on Singapore's land area as at end-June.

Data on population from 2003 onwards exclude residents who have been away from Singapore for a continuous period of 12 months or longer as at the reference period.

Source: SingStat, Century 21 (IPA)

Figure 2: HDB towns and their projected target of dwelling units

HDB towns	Land size (Ha)	Flats under HDB management	Projected ultimate number of units
Ang Mo Kio	638	49,169	58,000
Bedok	937	60,115	79,000
Bishan	690	19,664	34,000
Bukit Batok	785	32,275	53,000
Bukit Merah	858	51,885	68,000
Bukit Panjang	489	34,463	44,000
Choa Chu Kang	583	42,393	62,000
Clementi	412	25,480	39,000
Geylang	678	29,256	49,000
Hougang	1,309	51,646	72,000
Jurong East	384	23,379	30,000
Jurong West	987	71,755	94,000
Kallang/Whampoa	799	35,740	57,000
Pasir Ris	601	29,207	44,000
Punggol	975	35,515	96,000
Queenstown	694	30,546	60,000
Sembawang	708	20,311	65,000
Sengkang	1,055	59,497	92,000
Serangoon	737	21,293	30,000
Tampines	1,200	66,599	110,000
Toa Payoh	556	36,439	61,000
Woodlands	1,198	62,675	98,000
Yishun	788	56,698	84,000
Other Estates	-	22,856	25,000
Total		968,856	1,504,000
		To be built	535,144

"Toa Payoh" town includes Bidadari

"Other Estates" include Bukit Timah, Central Area and Marine Parade

Land size includes private developments on private and state land. Projected ultimate figures include private developments under Government Land Sales Programme.

Source: HDB "Key Statistics – HDB Annual Report 2014/15", Century 21 (IPA)

land sales for private residences, are also listed. Do note that the projected ultimate number does not include residences that will be built on private land, or en bloc redevelopments of apartments on state land.

From the differences in the totals, we see that sufficient land has been set aside to build another 535,144 dwelling units in the next decade and beyond. However, these units reside purely within HDB towns, and various large private residential estates such as Bukit Timah, Newton-Novena, Tanglin and the Downtown Core have not been included.

New Residential Precincts — An Additional 534,000 Units?

In the past 10 years, announcements have been made regarding new residential precincts such as Woodlands North Coast, Jurong Lake District, Tampines North and Bidadari. The additional housing capacity planned in these new precincts have been included in the projected ultimate numbers listed under the HDB towns of Woodlands, Jurong East, Tampines and Toa Payoh in Figure 2.

In addition, there are four more new residential precincts that are being planned. The operations in Paya Lebar Air Base will cease from 2030 onwards and we may expect the first HDB flats to begin construction perhaps two years later. The advantage this brings to the immediate neighbourhoods such as Hougang and Aljunied is that height restrictions may be lifted and plot ratios increased significantly.

Fancy being a resident of Pulau Brani? The Greater Southern Waterfront will begin its transformation from 2027, when the City Terminals start to relocate to Tuas, followed by the Pasir Panjang Terminal around year 2030.

Tengah could be named as a new HDB town when details of its plans are revealed. This precinct has been set aside in the Master Plans for some time now and with the recently announced plans to develop the new Jurong Innovation District, plans for the Tengah new town could be accelerated.

The overall plans for Marina South Residential District was crystallised starting from a design competition held in 2007. Plot ratios assigned to the residential blocks at "Gardenfront Residences" are relatively high at between 4.9 and 5.6, allowing the lucky residents to have a clear view over the Supertrees in Gardens by the Bay.

Figure 3: Estimates of the total housing units that will be built in four new residential precincts that were previously announced and included in the Master Plans 2008 and 2014. The estimate for the 9,000 housing units in Marina South is stated on the Urban Redevelopment Authority's website and the other estimates are based on the author's estimates based on various sources.

New Residential Precincts	Land Size (Ha)	Estimated Housing Units	Estimated Start Date
Paya Lebar Air Base	800	120,000	2032
Greater Southern Waterfront	1,000	150,000	2030
Tengah	700	55,000	2017
Marina South	60	9,000	2018
Others	n.a.	200,000	2050?

Source: URA, Century 21 (IPA)

Besides the above, scanning the Master Plan 2014, we will see that there are large tracts of land available in Sungei Kadut, Simpang, Lim Chu Kang, etc, which are available for building 200,000 more residences from 2050 and beyond.

Increasing Plot Ratio, Improving Space Planning

Intensifying land use and increasing population density are made possible through several elements. Plot ratios across the country can be increased due to better planning and integration with public transportation and changing lifestyles. Examples can be seen from the rebuilding of old estates such as Commonwealth, Tanglin and Dawson where old 10-storey blocks with open-air car parks were demolished and replaced with new 40-storey blocks that are built closer and integrated with amenities such as multi-storey car parks, clinics, supermarkets and community facilities to boot.

In private housing, apartment sizes are shrinking, especially when the increase in single person households support the proliferation of shoebox units. The smaller average size of apartments has led to an increase of about 20% more residential units than what is planned for each parcel of government land sold.

Looking Forward

The current total stock of residential units exceeds 1.3 million and together with alternative accommodation types such as dormitories and serviced apartments, Singapore can comfortably house 5.54 million people. Based on the tabulations in the sections above, I believe that Singapore has sufficient capacity to add 1.1 million more housing units without further reclamation of land. We can then comfortably welcome another 4.5 million people.

In this whole discussion, we have not yet included innovative new solutions that the government is testing out in creating additional space underground for an entire network of factories, logistics facilities and warehouses.

Someone recently said, "With inflation, the rising cost of living and land scarcity, property prices will continually rise in Singapore over time, which makes property a great investment." I think he will be correct, provided we can continue to keep the population growing. But be careful of yet another misconception: thinking that we are forever attractive to immigrants.

10. Time to Take Action on Real Estate Policies

30 September 2016, TODAY

Structural changes, market shifts and policy changes are taking place in the real estate sector. Many of these are subtle, incremental changes, but they have the potential to one day pull the rug from under our feet, shrinking the demand for real estate significantly. We should begin to openly acknowledge their impact and contemplate how to tackle the challenges.

In the retail sector, the rise of e-commerce, a weak consumer market and changing preferences have finally tipped the sector over the cliff. Vacant retail space increased from 3.7 million sqft (or 5.9% vacancy rate) in 2Q2014 to 5.0 million sqft (or 7.8%) in 2Q2016. As banks and point of sales systems go cashless and FinTech spreads its wings, banks will consolidate their retail branch network, reducing demand for retail space.

FinTech, especially developments in blockchain technology, will also lead to a reduction of jobs in the banks' middle and back offices, as well as in accounting, auditing, and other transaction-processing roles. Over the next few years, with the widespread adoption of such technologies and new business practices, we may expect a net reduction in demand for office and business park space.

Co-working is another business trend impacting the demand for traditional office spaces. A co-working space is more efficient in layout and results in better utilisation of floor area than a traditional office. For example, a 5,000 sqft co-working space might fit up to 100 office workers from many different companies, whereas a traditional office of of the same size might be occupied by only one company with 30 staff. In other words, 1 sqft of co-working space could cannibalise 3 sqft of traditional office space. In locations where retail rents are cheap, co-working spaces are beginning to coexist with coffee bars and food outlets. Expect the overall demand for office space to shrink as co-working spaces flourish.

We pride ourselves on having one of the highest home-ownership rates in the world. Yet, in a fast-changing global economy where venture capital and entrepreneurship are highly valued, we happily lock away our precious capital in properties, chained by 30-year mortgages. A dozen property cooling measures in the last six years have managed to flatten both the HDB resale index and the URA Private Property Index — but the market has not stabilised.

While we think that buyers have come to their senses, more than a dozen families paid over $1 million for public housing units in 2016. Construction materials now cost less, but the prices for new public housing have been kept steady — in fact, price records were set for new flats in Bidadari. With the slowdown in household income growth, public housing may become less affordable. In the private residential market, 99-year leasehold condominiums in hyped up growth areas in the outskirts transact at $1400 per sqft, similar to freehold condominiums along River Valley Road in prime District 9. It seems that we attract speculators, not long-term investors.

But structural changes in the real estate scene pale in comparison to the seismic shifts that Singapore's economy is facing. Singapore used to attract expatriates with an abundance of jobs, the availability of good education for children, and the offer of a safe and clean environment, where infrastructure operate smoothly and run like Swiss clockwork. Local and foreign investors alike loved to invest in our quality private properties for the long-term store of value and steady rental returns.

Today, job creation has slowed. Our biggest strengths have turned into our biggest millstones. We used to hold dominant positions in the oil and gas industry, enjoyed significant global market share in the offshore and marine industry and was a key player in global trade and container shipping. The risks-rewards balance of these industries are tilted against us now. The hub-and-spoke entrepot trade model served us well in the past, as we were more efficient and had better infrastructure than many others in Asia. Today, a persistent decline in global trade coupled with cheap shipping and air freight rates made point-to-point logistics more efficient.

As economic prospects dim, the number of expatriates coming in are fewer than the number of residential units we are completing. Although the indices do not show it, rents are dropping fast. Affected by the weak market outlook and a shaky job market, consumer spending drops too as property owners tighten their belts in order to pay mortgages. Most high net worth investors have shunned the property market. Yet, public housing prices are scoring record highs at $1.1 million, while 99-year leasehold residences in the outskirts are sold at prime district dollar per sqft prices.

These show that policy measures have not worked as well as we have hoped. Public housing needs to remain affordable, not setting record-high prices. Investment-grade private residences in prime District 9 and District 10 should not be suppressed to mass market values.

Perhaps we have been looking inwards a little too much and have lost sight of the long-term sustainability of Singapore's wealth. Real estate is the bedrock of Singapore's economy and today, this bedrock has been weakened by severe oversupply and a discriminatory exclusion of foreigners from investing in luxury residences.

One way to restore the lopsided situation back to normalcy would be to welcome institutional and high net worth investors back to Singapore's luxury residences in District 9 and 10. Otherwise, we might lose this category of investors for the long term as the image of Singapore's luxury properties being unworthy of their investment sets in.

The oversupply of properties islandwide hurts the market. We would be wise to place all future government land sales under the Reserve List, save for certain sites which are deemed strategic imperatives in the Master Plan.

This is a race against time. We should quickly acknowledge the structural shifts in the real estate market and take immediate steps to bolster the bedrock before we fall over the cliff.

11. Drop in Private Housing Vacancy Rate Confounds

4 November 2016, TODAY

The much anticipated annual publications Population in Brief 2016, Population Trends 2016, the Housing & Development Board's (HDB) Key Statistics 2016 and the data from the third quarter of 2016 for the entire property market provided a lot of numbers for analysts to chew on.

In addition, a report published on 20 October 2016 by Mr Sai Min Chow and Mr Royston Tan from Nomura Singapore Ltd, titled "Addressing five half-truths", categorically debunked residential sector hoopla using plain market data which the market ignored. These were the five questions straightened out: (1) Was there a robust pick-up in private home sales? (2) Has the demand for prime luxury homes risen? (3) Is the unsold inventory low, especially in the suburbs? (4) Has private housing vacancies peaked? (5) Has the prime luxury segment bottomed?

While most indicators, such as the rental and price indices, in the 3Q2016 reports published by the Urban Redevelopment Authority (URA) fell, there was one set of data which stood out as the only green dot in a sea of red: the increase in occupancy rate by 0.2%. In other words, there was a decline in the private residential vacancy which, to me, was a major surprise.

According to the URA, the total stock of private residential units at the end of 3Q2016 stood at 343,647, with 29,836 units sitting vacant. This implies that 313,811 units are occupied. In the previous quarter, the total stock of private residences was 338,728 units, with 30,310 uninhabited units and 308,418 occupied units.

So while the total stock increased by 4,919 units due to the completions of about two dozen projects, the total number of private residences occupied increased by 5,393 units. This lowers the vacancy rate from 8.9% to 8.7%, from the second to the third quarter of 2016.

Population Increase vs Dwelling Units Take-Up Rate

The drop in vacancy rate due to the large take-up of private residential units looks odd given that data from population growth and other indicators such as a contraction in total employment and weak macroeconomic numbers should lead one to think that vacancy rates would rise.

According to the Population in Brief 2016 report, the categories contributing to the 72,300 population growth were 33,700 new births (possibly due to a very successful SG50 celebration package), foreign domestic workers and the "dependents of Singaporeans who are on Long-Term Visit Passes".

Population growth from these three categories is unlikely to amount to any significant take-up of private housing units. Furthermore, during the third quarter, an additional 1,535 units of Executive Condominiums (ECs) were also occupied. While we have no clear quarterly data on the stock of HDB flats and their occupancy rates, we can assume that the 25,000 additional HDB flats added to the total stock in 2016 will be occupied (or 6,250 per quarter), due to the mandatory minimum occupation period rule. That is, during the third quarter of 2016, Singapore saw a take-up of 5,393 private residential units, 1,535 EC units and possibly 6,250 HDB flats.

Where did these households come from to take-up more than 13,000 dwelling units in a single quarter? New household formation,

Figure 1: Singapore population increase versus the take-up of private residences, ECs and the increase in the stock of HDB flats

	Annual population increase*	Annual take-up of private residential units**	Annual take-up of ECs**	Annual increase in HDB flats***
2011	107,000	7,428	- 31	11,759
2012	128,700	9,963	41	14,871
2013	86,800	8,616	188	7,887
2014	70,500	13,385	2,730	16,142
2015	65,300	16,179	3,490	27,985
2016 (till 30 Sept)	72,300	12,880	3,180	23,616
- 1Q2016	n.a.	4,453	654	n.a.
- 2Q2016	n.a.	3,034	991	n.a.
- 3Q2016	n.a.	5,393	1,535	n.a.

* Data published as of 30 June every year

** Data based on 31 December every year

*** Data based on 31 March every year

n.a. = not available

Sources: Department of Statistics, URA, HDB, IPA

referenced against the 10-year average (2005–2015) of 21,900 marriages per year, or 5,475 per quarter, may explain about 40% of the take-up. But that is if we assume that all newly-wedded couples move immediately into an independent dwelling after marriage.

To add to the demand for housing, we may also consider the roughly 7,000 divorces and annulments every year (or 1,750 per quarter), as well as assume that more singles are moving out to live on their own. But I am still unable to explain about 30% of the 13,000 take-up in a single quarter.

The Art of Determining Vacancy

In Figure 1 above, the increase in take-up refers to the increase in the number of dwelling units that are occupied. This is derived from the total stock less the number of vacant units. However, estimating the number of vacant houses, apartments and ECs is challenging. As it will be too laborious and impractical to survey the entire stock of over 300,000 private residences to find out how many are vacant, URA carries out regular surveys based on the sampling of several thousand addresses across the spectrum of residential types and districts.

With the random sample of addresses, URA reviews the corresponding utilities bills of these houses, apartments and ECs to determine if they may be occupied, or vacant. A dwelling unit is considered "occupied" if, based on its size and property type, its total utilities bill has exceeded a certain level. For example, a three-bedroom condominium unit with 1,300sqft of strata area showing a monthly utilities bill of over $250 will be classified as "occupied" but a three-bedroom terrace house with a bill of less than $50 per month is probably vacant. For cases which may be unclear, URA representative may visit the properties to confirm their findings.

Given that vacancy rates, or the number of occupied dwelling units, are estimated through sampling household utilities bills, it is clear that we should not make conclusions on take-up rates by relying on a single quarter of data. Based on my daily work as a property agent, I would think that the number of vacant units is likely to be 10–15% higher than what the official data suggests.

In view of the supply of more than 120,000 dwelling units in the next three years against the slowing employment and population growth, we should pay close attention to the trend of take-up rates to better understand the risks of residential rentals.

Author's Note

After this article was published, the URA clarified that they have enhanced their methodology to estimate vacancy rates. Since the fourth quarter of 2016, the survey has been widened to cover the utilities consumption of all completed private residential units. This removes some of the errors that may arise due to sampling. I am confident that the improved survey method will provide better confidence about the vacancy data. Since the article was written and up to 2Q2017, 12,469 private residences were added to the country's total stock and an additional 13,417 units were occupied. Given the shrinkage in employment, the reduction of foreign workers and the declining rentals, I remain puzzled as to where the occupiers of these units came from.

12. From Scarcity Comes Bargaining Power

The article was co-authored with Justina Joseph Steven, a research intern from Ngee Ann Polytechnic.

6 January 2017, TODAY

Our forecast for residential prices to drop by 8–10% in 2016 was off the mark. The Urban Redevelopment Authority's (URA) private residential index turned out surprisingly resilient, dropping a mere 3.0% for the whole year, while the HDB resale price index ended the year almost where it began.

While it looks like the policy measures have managed to stabilise prices in the residential market, a deeper look at the numbers reveal that the overall B-grade result was achieved through A grades in a couple of subjects and B, C and D grades in other subjects. Examining the performance of the various regions and sub-types, such as landed housing, we might conclude that 2016 was a directionless market.

Several factors point to a continued search for direction in 2017.

On the One Hand, Upward Pressure on Price Indices

More than a dozen HDB flats transacted above the $1 million mark in 2016 and many more set new area records of above $900,000 in the resale market to push up the HDB resale index.

Developers have also contributed to the upward shift in the

private residential price index. For example, a few projects which have gone quiet for more than a year started selling briskly when developers offered discounts and attractive payment schemes. Even with the discounts, the prices achieved for these relatively new apartments were higher than the average prices in their respective neighbourhoods, nudging the index upwards.

Monetary Authority of Singapore (MAS) and Inland Revenue Authority Singapore (IRAS) have proposed regulations, and as of 1 January 2017, implemented the Common Reporting Standard (CRS) with 46 countries. The first Automatic Exchange of Information (AEOI) will commence in 2018. This is an agreement among participating countries to share information about residents' gross financial assets, a move to deter and detect tax evasion through the use of offshore bank accounts. The key element in the exchange is to disclose the value of the high net worth individual's bank accounts.

Some foreign high net worth individuals might not feel at all comfortable with the disclosure of the value of their accounts to their home country's taxman. We might, therefore, expect a fraction of them to trade their financial assets for other "real assets" like luxury properties.

It seems that there is plenty of liquidity amongst high net worth investors and prudent owner-occupiers who have not placed their property bets in the frothy market three years ago. And perhaps the above are reasons why the government is reluctant to relax any cooling measures.

On the Other Hand, Abundant Downward Pressure

Investors who ran low on holding power have sold their properties with losses or defaulted on their mortgages. According to research by The Edge Property, the proportion of unprofitable deals rose from 10% (447 of 4,687) in 2015 to 17% (873 of 5,264) in 2016. These figures refer to resale transactions of condominium and apartments where the previous caveats can be traced.

Defaults on residential mortgages increased from 2014 through to 2016 and are likely to increase further as retrenchments and vacancies increase, rentals decline and interest rates rise in 2017.

Developers avoiding penalties imposed for not selling out their new projects will probably slash prices for bulk investment deals, and offer attractive payment schemes and stamp duty absorption to clear the remaining units.

Adding to the pressure is an increasing supply in the second-hand market. An increasing number of families who treat HDB flats as investments are eligible to sell their flats after the five-years Minimum Occupation Period (MOP). Thus, resale values have declined, especially those in less desirable locations of Singapore, such as five-room flats in Choa Chu Kang, Jurong West, Punggol, Sengkang and Woodlands.

Figure 1: Median resale prices of five-room HDB flats in Choa Chu Kang, Jurong West, Punggol, Sengkang and Woodlands from 1Q2012 to 3Q2016.

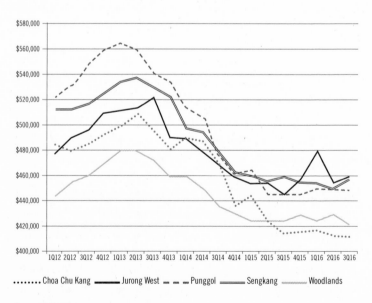

Source: HDB, IPA

The situation is similar for Executive Condominiums (EC) which has a MOP of five years, and for private residences which are "discharged" from the four-year Seller's Stamp Duty (SSD) liability. Due to the massive ramp up in residential developments post-Lehman Crisis, the supply of resale HDB flats, ECs and private homes are expected to increase in the next few years, pressuring prices further down.

Figure 2: We may expect a steady increase in resale transactions for both public and private housing as more HDB flats and ECs complete their Minimum Occupation Periods and more private properties are "discharged" from the four-year SSD liability.

	Additional HDB and DBSS flats#	New HDB and DBSS flats crossing five-year MOP	Number of private residential transactions	Number of private residences passing the four-year SSD mark	Number of additional ECs	Number of ECs crossing five-year MOP
2010	6,316	–	–	–	0	–
2011*	11,759	–	32,640	–	0	–
2012	14,871	–	37,873	–	0	–
2013	7,887	–	22,719	–	1,253	–
2014	16,142	–	12,847	–	3,357	–
2015	27,985	6,316	14,117	32,640	3,296	–
2016	23,616	11,759	16,000^	37,873	4,560^	–
2017	–	14,871	–	22,719	–	0
2018	–	7,887	–	12,847	–	1,253
2019	–	16,142	–	14,117	–	3,357
2020	–	27,985	–	16,000^	–	3,296
2021	–	23,616	–	–	–	4,560^

 # Figures obtained from HDB annual reports for years ending 31 March are net additional flats, excluding the units demolished under the Selective En bloc Relocation Program. The actual number of new flats added is higher.

* The four-year SSD was implemented on 14 January 2011

^ IPA's estimates

Source: HDB, URA, IPA

This is good news for buyers who are looking for good-value picks. Property agents may also celebrate the potentially higher transaction volumes.

A Two-Tier Market Looms

Barring seismic shifts from global political and economic events, what might happen when the upward pressure of excess liquidity combine with the potential increase of resale residences? 2016 presented us with a hint of the answer: a two-tier market will develop in both the public and the private housing segment.

We may expect the massive supply and weak rental demand in the outskirts of Singapore to bring prices down. Meanwhile, cash-rich investors looking for gems in the market will focus on centrally located properties. We believe that this trend will continue for the next three years and price gaps will widen.

As the market waits out the supply glut to be absorbed through population growth, investors might do well to appoint a diligent property agent to sift out the well-built, undervalued, freehold private residences in Districts 9 and 10. When the next economic boom hits Singapore, the value of these properties will simply jump. Bargaining power is enhanced by scarcity.

13. Counting the Love of Aircon Ledges in Dollars

13 February 2017, TODAY

Just how much do investors pay for air-conditioner (AC) ledges every year? A whopping $780 million.

I hope my estimates are wrong, but simply examining new residential sales in the six years from 2011 to 2016, it seems that we have invested a total of $4.7 billion in AC ledges. If we included another 3% of normal buyer stamp duties and disregarded the buyers who have paid additional buyer stamp duties of as much as 15%, the stamp duties collected on these AC ledges exceeded $140 million.

In this article, I have not included the larger AC ledges sold with strata industrial, retail or office units, which were investors' darlings following the series of residential cooling measures imposed from 2010 to 2013. The strata retail and strata office units have generally higher unit prices than residential properties, ranging from $3,000 to $10,000 per sqft, meaning that a 50 sqft AC ledge of a strata retail shop priced at $8,000 per sqft is an investment of $400,000 for the buyer, excluding stamp duty.

What is the issue?

There is nothing wrong with investors buying oversized AC ledges.

However, most investors probably do not realise that they have bought overly large, unusable areas for collecting dirt. Worse, astute tenants will bargain for rents that commensurate with usable spaces. Question: For which 700 sqft apartment do you think a tenant would be more willing to pay a rental of $2,500 a month: one that has a 54 sqft AC ledge or one that has a 21 sqft AC ledge?

Ancillary areas such as ledges, planters, voids, patios and balconies are usually discounted by tenants when it comes to rental price bargaining. The net usable area is especially important to tenants of strata industrial, retail and office units as they will only consider commercially productive floor areas.

How much is too much?

The typical footprint for an AC compressor that can cool three rooms is no more than 3 sqft and a high capacity model for residential use that can cool up to five rooms simultaneously has a footprint of less than 4 sqft.

Figure 1 below shows the breakdown of areas for a medium-sized and a small-sized two-bedroom unit in Condominium A and Condominium B respectively. Assuming that the owners like really cold temperatures, they might install two small-sized AC compressors with footprints of about 2–3 sqft each and install five indoor units to cool the two bedrooms, living room, dining room and kitchen. Without having to stack up the compressors and allowing for better access for maintenance and repairs, a 20 sqft AC ledge should be more than sufficient.

However, as Figure 1 shows, the investors each paid $107,600 for 53.8 sqft of AC ledges, more than half of which is unnecessary. Add to that the stamp duties and interest expenses and the total cost is sufficient to keep a small business going for many months.

Buyer Beware

The issue really boils down to the often quoted Latin phrase "Caveat Emptor", which is the principle that investors alone

Figure 1: Illustration of the proportion of AC ledges for a single-floor, two-bedroom apartment in Condominium A and Condominium B. Both city-fringe projects were sold at about $2,000 per sqft.

	Condominium A	Condominium B
Total strata area (sqft)	1,001.1	710.4
Balcony area (sqft)	161.5	75.3
AC ledge size (sqft)	53.8	53.8
Interior area which requires cooling (sqft)	785.7	581.3
AC ledge as a proportion of total strata area	5.4%	7.6%
AC ledge as a proportion of interior area which requires cooling	6.8%	9.3%
Cost of AC ledge @ $2,000 per sqft	$107,600	$107,600
Footprint of AC compressor required	Up to 10 sqft	Up to 10 sqft

take responsibility for checking on the investment target before committing to the investment. However, the $4.7 billion bill for new AC ledges over the last six years indicates that investors do not know that they have overpaid for concrete slabs. They are only aware of the poor investment value when they are unable to achieve their expected rental returns.

To derive the total value of AC ledges sold by developers every month, we downloaded the new sales of private residences and Executive Condominiums from January 2011 to December 2016, and based on my observations in showflats in the past few years, I assume that the average size of AC ledges in these residential units is 40 sqft. Then we multiply:

- the number of units sold in each project each month,
- the median per sqft price transacted for that project during that month, and
- 40 sqft of AC ledge per residential unit.

You can see from Chart 1 the value of new AC ledges sold every month for the past 6 years.

Figure 2: Value of AC ledges sold monthly

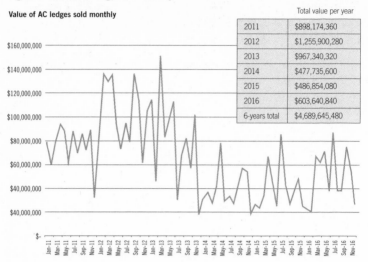

Value of AC ledges sold monthly

	Total value per year
2011	$898,174,360
2012	$1,255,900,280
2013	$967,340,320
2014	$477,735,600
2015	$486,854,080
2016	$603,640,840
6-years total	$4,689,645,480

What Is a Suitable Size for an AC Ledge?

The government does not mandate sizes for AC ledges to guide developers and architects. Rightly so because we would loath for the strong hand of government to be involved in nitty gritties such as 40 sqft ledges. I believe that any professional architect can calculate how many AC compressors are required to cool the interior air volume of any homes which they design, and plan for suitably-sized AC ledges.

However, oversized AC ledges are prevalent today because while the area of AC ledges of up to one metre (or 3.3 feet) width do not count towards the Gross Floor Area (GFA) and Plot Ratio of a condominium development, they are considered strata area which developers can sell. Overvalued AC ledges is one of several examples where the distortion between the definitions of GFA and strata area is costing investors and yielding inferior financial returns.

Prescription: Re-classify Strata Area to Exclude AC Ledges

Since May 2012, the government has mandated developers to provide prospective buyers with clearly marked floor plans of the units with detailed breakdown floor areas such as bedrooms, kitchens, living rooms, AC ledges and balconies. Buyers should be able to make informed decisions before taking out their chequebooks. However, these measures apparently did not help buyers open their eyes any wider as investments into new AC ledges in residences totalled almost a billion dollars in 2013.

I believe that the real answer to a suitable size for an AC ledge will emerge once we re-classify the AC ledge as a non-strata-area such that developers and architects will design cool homes with better investment value. In the more developed real estate markets such as Japan and Australia, because AC ledges are not strata sellable areas, AC compressors are simply stacked and tucked into the side of a balcony. Easy to maintain. Less wasted space.

To tackle the problem at its root, it is imperative that we address the chasm in the definitions of "GFA" and "strata area" so as to prevent future investors from overpaying for unusable and non-productive areas such as AC ledges, advertising ledges, external void areas and internal void areas. This will be a mammoth task requiring the coordination between various government departments as the responsibility for defining strata area comes under the Singapore Land Authority and the Ministry of Law while GFA and other related planning and development control guidelines come under the purview of the Urban Redevelopment Authority and the Ministry of National Development.

I hope the twain shall meet. Soon.

14. Helping First-Timer Families While Hindering Entrepreneurship

The long-awaited report from the Committee for the Future Economy (CFE) was finally released in February 2017 and as expected, a key recommendation (Recommendation 7.2) was for the government to "create a regulatory environment to support innovation and risk-taking".

Paragraph 143 explained that "Our processes and regulations have provided a safe and predictable environment for our people and enterprises, but have grown established and less flexible over time. The Government will need to be nimbler given the rapid pace of innovation and increasing global competition. We must take risks and be willing to make fundamental changes to support the emergence of potentially-disruptive business activities."

We were told to expect a Singapore Budget 2017 that supports the recommendations of the CFE. So I was surprised to hear the Minister for Finance announcing in the Budget Statement on 20 February 2017 that first-timer families buying resale HDB flats will be given more CPF Housing Grants: $50,000 if a family bought four-room or smaller flats (an increase of $20,000), and $40,000 for buying flats of five-rooms or larger flats (an increase of $10,000).

Note that grants for first-timer families buying resale HDB flats are already rather generous. First-timers buying a flat near to their parents or their married child are eligible for the $20,000 Proximity Housing Grant. Those with monthly incomes of below $5,000 can get Additional CPF Housing Grants of between $5,000 and $40,000. With the increased CPF Housing Grants given, each first-timer family may receive up to a total of $110,000.

Following the positive news for first-timers in the Budget Statement, new measures were announced at the Ministry of National Development's Committee of Supply debate on 7 March 2017, where first-timer families could get their keys to BTO and balance flats more quickly.

Does the budget support the recommendations of the CFE or will it actually hamper our desire to support innovation? Why the generosity towards first-timers?

The Budget Statement made utilities more costly so as to generate more revenue to balance the budget. The rapidly declining employment market clearly indicates that we need to step up on job creation. Hence I find it odd that "an additional $110mil per year" was budgeted to beef up the already generous grants for first-timers to buy resale flats.

Additional grants for home purchases merely add to taxpayers' burden without bringing wider economic benefits and multipliers. The likely result is: instead of buying BTO flats, Executive Condominiums or private properties, hundreds of first-timer families will buy resale flats simply for the increased grants. We would also be mistaken to think that the additional grants will hasten the pace of marriage and parenthood. The spin-offs to the economy are probably limited to conveyancing fees and property agents' fees.

The Downside of Excessive Welfare

Most first-time home buyers do not calculate the financial risks and constraints when jumping into such expensive commitments. Many are not concerned about the fact that CPF grants and monies withdrawn to pay for their flats need to be repaid with interest when the flats are sold.

Current home information	
Purchase price	$400,000
Financing details	
a. Cash outlay for 5% down payment	$20,000
b. Initial CPF outlay for 15% down payment	$60,000
Stamp duty	$6,600 Assuming CPF is used to pay
Legal fees @ 1.5%	$6,000
Total CPF outlay	$72,600
c. Bank loan:	
Loan Tenure	25 years
Interest Rate	2% p.a monthly compounding
Loan amount	$320,000
Monthly debt service	$1,356 (Financed using CPF)
Sale of home	
Selling price	$450,000
a. CPF refund (with accrued interest)	
From lump sum withdrawal	$93,196
From monthly withdrawal	$184,695
Total CPF refund	$277,891
b. Loan balance @ EOY 10	$210,772
c. Agent fees @ 2%	$9,000
Total amount to be paid	$497,662
Amount of cash to be forked out	$47,662

Let us take the example of Mr and Mrs Tan, who took advantage of the increased CPF grants and bought a $400,000 resale four-room flat in Sengkang with 5% cash and 15% CPF funds for down payment. They would be servicing the 25-year bank mortgage with monthly CPF contributions.

Meanwhile, we can be certain that the future economy will be more turbulent. Job tenures will shrink as the pool of temporary and contract employees grow. Therefore, this is a likely scenario in 10 years' time: Mr and Mrs Tan would have to sell their flat due to the retrenchment of the sole breadwinner.

Given the flat's older age and the relatively urgent nature of the sale, they are probably happy to settle for a small profit and sell the property in order to downsize. (In fact, by 2027, we may expect competition in the resale HDB market to be very stiff: more than half a million retired baby boomers who are over 70 years of age will be in divestment mode.) Still, let us be optimistic and assume that Mr and Mrs Tan managed to sell their flat at $450,000.

We have, on paper, a gross profit of $50,000. However, this resale flat turns out to be a net loss after deducting the selling agent's fees of $9,000 (before goods & services tax), legal fees, relocation costs and 10 years of 2.0% per annum interest expenses of about $53,000.

Furthermore, the total sum withdrawn from CPF over the last 10 years will need to be returned with interest that would have been earned if the money remained in their CPF accounts. They need to return to their CPF accounts $66,600 withdrawn for down payment and stamp duty at the beginning, as well as the roughly $162,000 withdrawn over 10 years for mortgage payments. On top of that, they need to return more than $40,000 of accrued interest to the CPF, making the total CPF refund close to $278,000.

In fact, Mr and Mrs Tan will have to dip into their cash savings for about $48,000 if they sold their flat at $450,000 to downgrade. In the face of financial constraints, could the Tans only downgrade their home by forking out additional cash!?

Unstable Jobs Environment

The CFE report noted that the future world will be more turbulent. Paragraph 6 forewarned: "We are in an era of rapid technological change. Innovation cycles have shortened. New technologies can supplant entire industries, displacing all their workers, even as they create new opportunities."

The probability of young workers being made redundant before their tenth year of work rises with technological and value chain disruptions. So the scenario above where the first-timer family might be forced to sell their flat within 10 years of purchase, will simply replay more frequently in future.

It would be safe to say that young families locked up with 25-year mortgages are not likely to venture into start-ups or even choose to work for SMEs. Their first choice, especially if parenthood were in the picture, would be to work for large and seemingly low-risk companies, or the government.

Paragraph 11 of the CFE report started with "We cannot know which industries will succeed. What we do know is that Singapore must stay open to trade, talent and ideas, and build deep capabilities." The CFE recommended that Singaporeans be innovative and bold in making changes.

Recommendations to Increase Investment Capital

Giving more grants to encourage young families to own flats is a counter-productive to the aim of making Singaporeans more open to entrepreneurship and innovation. This is because home-ownership depletes the investment capital of these young families and drastically reduce their risk appetite for business ventures.

One bold housing solution for young families to raise business capital would be to provide a class of long-term rental HDB flats. HDB could administer these rental flats across Singapore by converting all the unsold new flats under the Sale of Balance Flats Scheme into rental flats, adding to the total stock available for rental progressively.

We should further allow CPF monies to be used for renting HDB flats. To make it easier for young families embarking on their parenthood journey, CPF grants could be given for young families to subsidise their HDB rents. The $50,000 CPF grant for first-timer families translates to almost three whole years of rental given that the average three-room HDB flat rents for $1,600 per month.

The benefits of such a radical change are many. Young families will have the assurance of a solid landlord and a comfortable abode to grow in. Their personal cash savings will grow, and monthly CPF contributions will continue to earn interests from the CPF Board. They will be able to accumulate capital, a part of which will find its way to spur innovation and entrepreneurship.

Such a move by our policy makers will demonstrate a willingness to be bold in overhauling policies which are irrelevant to the Future Economy. It will lend great support to CFE's call for Singaporeans, and the Singapore government, to be nimble-footed in "embracing new realities and creating new opportunities".

Author's Note

This article was not accepted for publication by several mainstream media. The editor of a research organization's blog page considered this article, but sent back a string of comments and questions, including a basic explanation to help me understand what the National Budget is meant for. I decided to withdraw the submission. I am not sure whether my standard of writing is not good enough, or perhaps this topic is too sensitive for public consumption.

PART 3

DEVELOPMENTS IN THE COMMERCIAL MARKET

15. Office Space: Where Do We Go from Here?

15 April 2016, TODAY

Given the changes in the economic winds, recent investors in the office segment must be scratching their heads over the wisdom of their decisions. With rentals dropping while vacancies and interest rates climb, profitability and cash flow are taking hard hits.

Guided by the Previous Master Plans

The recent revisions of our national Master Plans were intended for the office segment to be decentralised from the Central Business District (CBD). These additional clusters of office locations are designed to bring "quality jobs near homes" while relieving the transport infrastructure from over-congestion.

Following the success of the Tampines Regional Commercial Centre, Master Plan 2008 (MP2008) included new regional commercial centres in Paya Lebar Central and Jurong Lake District. Master Plan 2014 (MP2014) further expanded the commercial centres to include a very large expanse of land called the North Coast Innovation corridor, comprising the Woodlands Regional Centre which will be developed on 1 million square metres of land and the Punggol Learning Corridor and Creative Cluster. Plans were also made to expand the Downtown Core, with the Bugis-Ophir-

Rochor corridor east of Marina Centre and The Great Southern Waterfront west of Tanjong Pagar.

What Has Transpired Since?

Property investors, big and small, bet on any news that is remotely positive. Many have invested in the North Coast Innovation Corridor story by buying into properties in Woodlands, Yishun, Sembawang and Punggol. Adding fuel to the frenzy was the announcement that the future rail link to Johor will be connected to the Woodlands North station. Initially announced in 2010 to be completed by 2018, the Johor Bahru–Singapore Rapid Transit System (RTS Link) has been delayed several times over. As at the time of writing this article, the decision for the construction has not been signed off. I am of the opinion that the RTS Link may only be completed years after 2022. Similar stories were told about the potentially bright future of Jurong Lake District and Paya Lebar Central. Investors also piled on their bets there, investing in the surrounding residential, retail and industrial segments.

The fact is, since MP2008 and MP2014 were announced, we have seen less than 10 office development projects in the regional commercial centres. The Woodlands Regional Centre had one commercial site tendered out for office development in early 2014 and nothing else.

With so much commercial land to develop in so many locations, including sites in the fringe of Downtown Core, how are the planners to prioritise office space development in each of the regional commercial centres, or the downtown core, over another? Large corporate office users, developers and investors are similarly confused about the pace of development in each location. It is not surprising that we have seen the reversal of decisions by several major government organisations and large listed companies in their intended shift to Jurong Lake District and the one-north precinct.

Our discussions have not even included the commercial centres in Changi Business Park, Alexandra Tech Park and the Buona

Vista-one-north-Science Park precinct, where significant office and business park spaces are being added. Neither have we discussed the potential competition from Industrial B1 space designated for developers of FinTech and software applications. And what about the most recent addition to the office development foray: Jurong Innovation District?

Figure 1: Vacancy and supply of space in the Office, Business Park and Industrial (Multiple-User Factory) segments as of 4Q2015.

Office	4Q15
Islandwide vacancy rate	9.5%
Islandwide vacancy	7.7 million sqft
Upcoming supply	11.3 million sqft
Deadline for ABSD remission	11 January 2017
– in 2016	5.0 million sqft
– in 2017	1.7 million sqft
– in 2018	2.2 million sqft
Business Park	4Q15
Islandwide vacancy rate	15.9%
Islandwide vacancy	3.3 million sqft
Upcoming supply	2.1 million sqft
Industrial (Multiple-User Factory)	4Q15
Islandwide vacancy rate	12.8%
Islandwide vacancy	14.2 million sqft
Upcoming supply	11.3 million sqft

Source: URA, JTC, Century 21 (IPA)

Structural Changes Afoot

Industries which have been shrinking recently, such as oil and gas, offshore and marine, commodities, logistics, shipping and manufacturing, as well as the investment banks and financiers serving them, are giving up office space. On top of our weak economy and declining demand, there is a structural change in how office space is being used. Technological leaps such as FinTech, mobile apps and affordable robots are disrupting current industry practices and supply chains, impacting how businesses are run.

Forecasts by Barclays and Citibank indicated that FinTech companies will reduce the number of bank employees by between 30–50% within 10 years. Singapore's financial services industry will not be spared. Bankers could be limited to senior relationship managers and back-end data centre engineers, with the bulk of transaction processing and middle offices displaced by FinTech apps.

Technology start-ups prefer to interact closely with businesses in the same ecosystem, and therefore the recent office configuration, the co-working space, is in vogue. These companies share work spaces with other companies, drastically reducing the square footage of office space per headcount. Gone are the days when a manager works from a 100 sqft room furnished with a six-feet-wide desk and two chairs in front, or a director from a 150 sqft room with an eight-feet-wide desk and a small discussion table on the side. Co-working spaces and mobile workers require about 50 sqft per employee, down from the traditional rule-of-thumb parameter of "80–100 sqft per staff".

Where Do We Go from Here?

Ironically, if the regional commercial centres succeed, they will compound the demise of the CBD that is at risk of being hollowed out by FinTech. Just as having malls in the suburbs reduces the reasons for suburban dwellers to visit Orchard Road, the future occupants of the CBD will be limited to the largest corporations.

But the fact remains that bringing jobs closer to homes is not as easy as building homes nearer to jobs. Corporations are not as flexible in their choices of location as individual workers and their families are. Therefore, it might take decades of economic growth before the demand for the various regional commercial centres builds up sufficiently.

Still, if the planners were faithful to the Master Plans' designs for the regional commercial centres, even in a weak economic environment, sites for small-sized office buildings of around 300,000 sqft gross floor area should be launched for sale in Woodlands, Paya Lebar Central and Jurong East.

More urgently, in the face of structural changes in office usage, we should re-map the current patchwork of commercial centres, and ask how Singapore might boost business demand to fill the existing 11 million sqft of vacant office and business park space, as well as where we might find the users for the next 13 million sqft of office and business park space completing by 2018.

16. FinTech and the Decline of Office Sector

The article was co-authored with Justina Joseph Steven, a research intern from Ngee Ann Polytechnic

2 December 2016, TODAY

So much has been presented about the positives of FinTech — short for "financial technology". The opening statement of a recently released report by Capgemini stated that "the term 'FinTech' might be both the most over-hyped and under-estimated term the industry has seen in decades." It is probably similar in stature to the term "dotcom" around the turn of the century.

In the World FinTech Report 2017 published by Capgemini and LinkedIn in collaboration with Efma, FinTech companies are defined as new financial services firms that are less than five years old and have a relatively small but growing customer base.

Sifting through articles about FinTech

An online search for articles about FinTech returns millions of hits, and wading past the advertisements, we will find hundreds of thousands of articles about the benefits that this revolution will bring to the business world. Yet, I can scarcely find any write-ups about what the aftermath of a FinTech tsunami might look like.

Every bank talks about what they intend to do with FinTech. None of the banks talks about what FinTech will do to bankers. Save for a few high-profile predictions about the impact on jobs and the closure of bank branches, there is no serious analysis on the number of employees who will be made redundant, and the total floor area that will be given up by financial services firms, accounting firms, stock broking and trading companies, etc.

Reduction of the Banks' Retail Branches

Mr Antony Jenkins, former Group CEO of Barclays Bank, gave a speech in November 2015 titled *Approaching the "Uber Moment" in Financial Services: How Technology Will Radically Disrupt the Sector*. He predicted that "the number of branches and people employed in the financial services sector, as we view it today, may decline by as much as 50% over the next 10 years".

Citi Research agreed with the forecast, noting that Nordic banks have already halved the number of branches since the peak in 2009. In a report published in April 2016 titled "Digital Disruption: How FinTech is Forcing Banking to a Tipping Point", Citi Research added that they "believe that there could be another ≈30% reduction in staff during 2015–2025".

If these predictions came to pass in Singapore, and each of the local banks and foreign banks with Qualifying Full Bank licenses decided to close an average of 10 branches, we will see a reduction of 100 branches across Singapore. This translates to about a reduction of demand for 200,000 sqft of retail space and perhaps a redeployment of up to 3,000 branch-level bankers.

Office and Business Park Spaces

The bigger impact will be felt in the office property sector. Earlier this year, Morgan Stanley reported that blockchain technology, a component of FinTech, will make its biggest impact felt from the year 2020. When adopted extensively by banks and corporate users, post-trade settlement jobs, trade finance jobs and custodial services jobs will suffer most.

Other analysts have commented that with blockchain, the number of middle-office and back-office jobs in banks, as well as the need for auditors and accountants, will be reduced by 30–50%. It is not just the banks. Financial services firms and the insurance industry will be early beneficiaries of FinTech and are likely to follow the banks by taking advantage of technology to improve efficiency, streamline jobs and cut costs.

Estimating the numbers on the back of an envelope, financial services firms — including insurance, funds management, stockbroking, audit and accounting services — take up more than 20 million sqft of office and business park space across Singapore.

In the next 10 years, if FinTech delivers all the positives that are touted today and 30% of the jobs disappear, we might conceivably see banks and financial services firms reduce their office and business park spaces by 30%, or 6 million sqft.

Figure 1: 3Q2016 data for Office, Retail and Industrial sectors

	Vacant lettable floor area [sqft] (Vacancy Rate)	Total lettable floor area [sqft]	Upcoming supply in total gross floor area [sqft] (% of available floor space)
Office	8,568,100 (10.4%)	82,495,300	10,688,700 (13.0%)
Retail	5,489,600 (8.4%)	64,971,500	7,405,600 (11.4%)
Industrial			
– Business Park	4,348,700 (18.9%)	23,002,700	473,600 (2.1%)
– Multi-User Factory	14,531,400 (12.9%)	112,699,100	17,276,200 (15.3%)
– Single-User Factory	24,111,400 (9.4%)	256,323,100	20,193,300 (7.9%)

Source: URA, JTC, IPA

The current 8.6 million sqft of vacant office space, equivalent to 8.6 vacant blocks of Vivocity, is causing office rentals to slide as landlords compete for tenants in a weak economy. The upcoming supply of 10.7 million sqft in the next three years will add further pressure.

Cannibalisation from Industrial Space

Adding further pressure on the office sector are the trend of co-working spaces and the massive supply overhang of industrial space. Specifically, the multiple-user factory segment has 14.5 million sqft of vacant space (equivalent to 12.9% vacancy rate) and landlords desperate to secure tenants are competing hard with office landlords, offering light industrial space for less than half the rental value per sqft of space.

Many FinTech companies are qualified to rent light industrial space, and those who prefer cheaper locations often do. However, the competition for commercial tenants does not just stop with FinTech companies. Since the end of 2011, multiple-user factory spaces have increased by 20%, or almost 20 million sqft, and that has resulted in a wide variety of tenants, whose businesses are not always compliant with the intended light industrial purposes such as travel agencies, health spas, geomancy service providers, retailers, places of worship, etc.

Conclusion

Today's office sector is challenged by increasing vacancies, declining rentals and an onslaught of 10.7 million sqft of new offices that will be completed within the next three years. With FinTech's revolution in Singapore, vacancies and rentals are likely to worsen further. Cannibalisation from the 19 million sqft of vacant and 18 million sqft of soon-to-be-completed multiple-user factory and business park spaces will further weaken the demand for office space.

We should take immediate action in reviewing the office sector's challenges and needs before releasing more land for office development.

17. Retail Slump: When Will It Recover?

The article was co-authored with Feily Sofian, the Head of Research at The Edge Property.

2 May 2016, The Edge Property

The Department of Statistics Singapore released the February 2016 Retail Sales Index figures two weeks ago. The data shows that year-on-year, total retail sales value fell 3.2% from an estimated $3.5 billion in February 2015. The decline would have been bigger if not for the sales of motor vehicles, which increased 51% over February last year. On a year-on-year basis, retail sales excluding motor vehicles have been on a declining streak, with occasional blips.

The biggest contributor to the drop in retail sales was the food and beverage products category, which plunged 34.7%. The revenue or turnover of F&B services, such as cafés, fast food outlets, restaurants and caterers, dropped from an estimated $690 million in February 2015 to $677 million in February 2016, representing a 1.9% decline. Analysts reading these numbers should be forgiven for concluding that Singapore consumers are on a diet.

February 2016: An Extra Day, an Extra Event

February data poses additional challenges for analysts. The month usually has three fewer days than January and March, except for leap years when it has two fewer days. It is simpler to compare data year-on-year, but when it involves a leap year or when the Chinese New Year holidays fall in January, as they do occasionally, year-on-year comparisons become distorted.

There were 29 calendar days and 19 working days in February 2016, and 28 calendar days and 18 working days in February 2015. In percentage terms, that represents 3.6% and 5.6% more calendar and working days respectively in February 2016 than in February 2015.

Singapore hosts a major international exhibition once every two years. The Singapore Airshow was held on 16–21 February this year and according to the show statistics, there were 48,229 trade attendees, out of whom about 30% (about 14,000) were from overseas. The previous Singapore Airshow was held in February 2014.

February 2016 also saw an increase of 11.9% in the number of international visitor arrivals, or about 141,500 persons, over the February before. The additional day in the month and the Airshow contributed to the healthy increase in the tourism sector.

Given the three positive factors — an extra day in February 2016, the Airshow and the jump in international visitor arrivals — most market watchers expected an increase in retail spending over the same month in 2015. However, the cash registers in retail sales and F&B services collected $100 million less in February 2016.

Perhaps in trying to reverse the declining international visitor arrival numbers, the authorities have targeted higher headcount numbers by attracting mass market tourists instead of premium travellers. Marina Bay Sands and Resorts World Sentosa reported weaker revenues, lower profits and a drop in contribution from high rollers.

Another reason might be that the year kicked off on a weak note as a result of the turmoil in the oil and financial markets. Weak jobs data and increased layoffs probably led to belt-tightening.

Figure 1: Summary of vacancy rates, vacant floor space and pipeline supply of retail space

Retail segment	4Q15	1Q16
Overall vacancy rate	7.2%	7.3%
Overall vacant retail floor space, based on net lettable area (sqft)	4,639,284	4,725,396
Retail space under construction, based on gross floor area (sqft)	6,566,040	6,996,600
Total retail space planned and under construction, based on gross floor area (sqft)	8,977,176	8,611,200
Orchard Planning Area vacancy rate	7.6%	8.8%

Source: Urban Redevelopment Authorities, Century 21 (IPA)

For the whole of 2015, retailers gave up 323,000 sqft more space than they took up. Strong brands with solid financials in their home markets — such as FrancFranc, Rakuten, Lowry's Farm and Goods of Desire — closed their Singapore operations in the last two years. When reporting on these high-profile exits, news articles invariably quoted retailers and market watchers, blaming the poor retail performance on high rentals and expensive labour.

The retail rental index has declined gradually over the last six quarters by an average of 1% per quarter. Looking forward, we expect retail rentals to drop faster over the next 24 months owing to the closure of several significant brands and a large supply of new retail space.

Online Retailers Upping Their Game

Globally, the retail business is undergoing a major transformation and is causing many players to wither away. E-commerce players the likes of Amazon and Alibaba have taken market share from even the biggest international retailers. UK retailer BHS may go bankrupt while Kmart/Sears and Walmart have announced the closure of about 350 stores in the U.S. The retail scene in Singapore will not be spared.

While brick-and-mortar retailers are playing catch-up, online retailers continue to reinvent themselves. For example, more online retailers are offering delivery on Sundays. Not too long ago, Alibaba raised its stake in Singapore Post to enhance its logistic solutions and boost overseas revenue. Some online retailers are employing new technologies that allow customers to try on products digitally by entering their vital statistics, while others offer try-before-you-buy schemes.

Consumers are increasingly savvy when searching for the best deals online. With reliable, low-cost logistics, internet shopping will shrink the already small Singapore market further. An item of European clothing from a trusted brand can be sold at a 30% discount online, shipping charges included, compared with the same piece in a store on Orchard Road.

Tiny Market

The main reason retailers are not performing well is that the local consumer market is tiny. With the presence of e-commerce and Singaporeans travelling regularly overseas to shop, the market will shrink even more.

It is smaller than what we might expect of a population of 5.54 million. About 1.2 million are made up of foreign domestic workers, and student pass, S Pass and work permit holders, and their purchasing power is limited.

Many of the international retailers entered Singapore in 2011 and 2012, drawn by the growing population and Southeast Asia's economic boom. Population growth has, however, slowed down to around 1% per year over the past two years.

Singapore has also been touted as under-shopped in terms of its retail space per capita compared to Hong Kong. Hong Kong's retail sales value is nearly twice that of Singapore at HK$37 billion (S$6.4 billion) because of higher tourist arrivals and the local lifestyle.

Rental and Labour Costs Not Entirely to Blame

Most landlords are cognizant of the competition in the market and will reduce rentals when they cannot find tenants. So, if a retailer wants to take advantage of the shopper traffic and profile that a mall attracts, it has to pay the price asked. Otherwise, another retailer will take up the space.

In addition, while the tightening of foreign worker quotas has raised operating costs, this is not the crux of the problem. In fact, retail rents and labour costs in Singapore are only a fraction of those in Hong Kong. Rentals in Hong Kong are two to three times the per sqft price of an equivalent location in Singapore. Hong Kong's retail and restaurant workers are paid a minimum wage of HK$32.50 per hour, or about $1,276 a month assuming they work nine hours a day and 25 days each month. But the retail scene in Hong Kong is more vibrant than Singapore's.

The problems plaguing the local retail scene lie beyond rents and labour costs. Singapore's retailers need to examine their value propositions and reorganise their business practices around consumers' preferences. Many retailers simply operate a showroom, selling "me too" products and depend on the shopper traffic that the mall draws to move its goods. Such product pushers with no value-added services will lose out fast.

In comparison, take a look at Apple's flagship stores. They have an open-concept layout with about 10% of the total floor area used to display the brand's products. Apple plants the flagship stores in the world's most expensive real estate locations: Ginza in Tokyo, Regent Street in London, Fifth Avenue in New York and Rue de Rivoli in Paris. With only 10% of the space used to display products, the stores are dedicated to serving customers. Product sale is secondary, as most of its products are sold online and through direct sales channels such as schools and institutions.

Leading retail brands understand this point: When consumers step into your store, they want service, not just products. Products can be purchased online, usually at lower prices.

The flagship stores of Nike and Adidas are service-focused. The services include measuring a consumer's gait to determine which pair of shoes would be most suitable for his style of running. Such a service is difficult to order online, unless the consumer invests in the equipment for the necessary measurements. Cosmetics brands also understand this point well, and the leaders in this category train their frontline sales staff to be beauticians, and not simply order takers.

Retailers need to package their physical store products with excellent service, and provide a good customer experience and after sales service. Good in-store service, positive attitude of frontline staff and returns policy are among the factors that will draw customers back repeatedly.

Rents Will Be Compromised

Having said that, rents will naturally be compromised as the retail industry undergoes a massive restructuring. Brick-and-mortar retailers are expected to give up some physical store space as they adopt offline and online, or omnichannel strategies.

Malls are getting creative with their excess space and are evolving into social hubs that focus on customer experience. They are dedicating more space to play areas, KidZania-like edutainment, new-generation cinemas and concept stores. However, these spaces fetch lower rents on per sqft basis than if they were let out to small speciality stores.

On a more positive note, these new experiences may bring some lustre back to the retail market. They are also more sustainable alternatives than increasing F&B offerings. The latter might involve a lot of investment as F&B is a very competitive segment. In addition, their crowd-pulling capacity is restricted to lunch and dinner hours.

Some landlords have adopted new technologies to counter the soft retail market and rents. For example, the CapitaStar App is more than just a reward programme to retain customer loyalty; it is a tool to gain insight into customers' habits and preferences.

Finally, let us accept the fact that our market is tiny. The exit of retail brands will dull the local retail scene and compromise Singapore's position as a shopping destination, risking more leakage of shopping dollars overseas. Governments and landlords might wish to step up efforts to boost demand such as collaborating with travel agencies and extending discount vouchers for tourists. This would result in higher tourist dollars to make up for the tiny domestic market. Meanwhile, landlords and retailers should focus on how to increase demand for their products and services.

18. Retail Woes: Don't Blame the Landlords

15 July 2016, TODAY

It was the eve of a public holiday in early July. We were in the middle of the two-month-long Great Singapore Sale (GSS). Indonesia was also having a week-long Lebaran Holidays, when many Indonesian visitors were expected to descend on Singapore's shores to enjoy our good food and spend money in this shopping paradise.

Perhaps that was in the past, because on this evening, the department stores in Orchard Road were quiet. The shopper-void is especially stark given the GSS period and the holidays: ground floor, street-fronting retail space along Orchard Road, including eateries, were not half occupied. Orchard Road felt more vacant than on a normal work day in the middle of a busy work-week.

On social media, some concerned members of the public lambast commentators for pointing out the disease that is eating away at the retail scene. They would prefer commentators to suggest remedies instead of highlighting the vacant malls.

A well-known retailer blamed the high cost of rentals for crippling retailers. As an example, the retailer quoted that in 1988, shop rentals cost $9 per sqft per month while today the rentals are $35 per sqft per month.

Some landlords contend that they are forward-looking and progressing with the times: they organise festive events and promotions to drive traffic to their malls and try to maintain footfall. Others are more sensitive, explaining that they have done their best to attract retailers with more flexible rental agreements, but that the retailers are ultimately responsible for making their tills ring.

The fact that many shop lots sit empty could also be put down to the increase in new strata-titled malls in mixed development projects, the impact of e-commerce and the strong Singapore dollar.

What Are the Issues?

Singapore's retail market is ill, but we should not simply blame the landlords and the rental rates. In comparing the rental rates between 1988 and 2015, we should consider the market size for retailers. In 1988, Singapore's total population was 2.85 million and we welcomed about 4.1 million visitors. In 2015, our total population was 5.54 million and we had 15.2 million visitors. Singapore's consumer spending rose from around S$40 billion a year in 1988 to over S$130 billion a year in 2015.

The market size has more than tripled and that led to an increased demand for retail space; therefore, rentals increase.

Retail space exists in an open market where landlords compete hard for tenants at market-related prices. If a mall is overpriced relative to the footfall or the affordability of shoppers, rentals would have to drop in order to retain the retailers. The competition among landlords is stiff. But most retailers prefer the easy route: instead of creating products that will draw a beeline of consumers to their shops, they opt for malls with existing high traffic, which necessarily implies high rentals.

The Retail Market Will Weaken Further

A combination of negatives spells further hardship for retailers. Firstly, efficient and cheap logistics combined with trustworthy merchants and online payment systems are taking away the profits of traditional retailers that depend strongly on the walk-in traffic in the malls. Retailers who are pure product-pushers will be irrelevant once e-commerce and logistics merge.

Secondly, the strength of the Singapore dollar is allowing the middle- and upper-income earners to shop more when they travel to Malaysia, Australia, Indonesia and Japan. The UK was recently added to the list. In addition, products from overseas e-commerce portals are more attractively priced thanks to the favourable exchange rates. Exchange rates are not the only reason for attractive online prices. Better pricing and better discounts also contribute.

Thirdly, as we move into the "sharing economy", consumer expenditure is likely to reduce further as peer-to-peer exchange of products and money may not be captured.

The above factors have already contributed to a steady decline in consumer expenditure for the past two years. Year-on-year growth of the retails sales index has shown shrinkages in 20 out of the past 28 months.

Figure 1: Singapore's retail sales index (excluding motor vehicles) has shown a drop on a year-on-year basis for 20 out of the past 28 months.

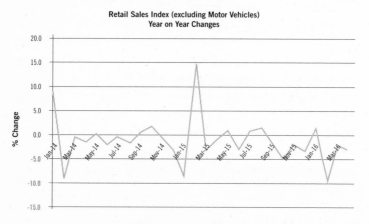

Source: SingStat, David Chien Zhong Xin, Century 21 (IPA)

Tourists are spending less too. Despite a growth of 0.9% in International Visitor Arrivals in 2015, the total tourism receipts fell by 7.6%. Put another way, each of the 15.2 million foreign visitors in 2015 spent an average of $1,434 during their time in Singapore, down 8.2% from the $1,563 per visitor in 2014.

The drops in retail sales and tourism receipts were disappointing given that in 2015 Singapore hosted the Southeast Asian Games and ran a year-long 50th anniversary celebration with lots of goodies distributed to the masses.

How Might Retailers and Landlords Move Forward?

Landlords and industry bodies will do well to note the changes in consumer purchase patterns and work hand-in-hand with retailers to support their internet distribution strategies, product launches, in-store promotions, risk-reward sharing contracts, etc. Landlords may also want to examine if traffic flow within their malls is impeded by outdated and inefficient designs.

Policy makers should also be cognizant of the new retail scene. Future government land sales and applications for new developments should severely limit the space available for retail. Gone are the days when cities are measured by the number of square feet of retail space per capita population. Foreign theoretical constructs do not necessarily apply to our small market.

Retailers need to ask themselves: What is the reason for consumers to purchase from the stores instead of purchasing from competitors or from online stores? What is the quality of the in-store services that cannot be replicated online? What knowledge and service capabilities do the in-store sales teams have? Do we have a go-to-market strategy that integrates in-store sales and online sales?

It is imperative for retailers to revisit the basics of good retail practices: offer sound product knowledge and advice to clients, provide reliable after sales service, implement fair returns policies and ensure that your products are good value for money.

Likewise, landlords will have to overhaul the fundamentals of the way they operate and closely collaborate with their tenants to win over the consumers. There will be pain during this transformation, but standing still may prove fatal. We have had truffles and foie gras for too long. Let us get back to salted eggs and porridge.

19. Two Pills for Orchard Road's Ills

The article was co-authored with Soh Yun Yee, an undergraduate of the School of Design & Environment, National University of Singapore.

22 August 2017, STORM.SG

It is no longer a surprise to see large clusters of vacant shops in malls all over Singapore. The retail sales index has shown declines in 27 out of the 39 months from January 2014 to January 2017. Weak retail sales has resulted in retailers racking up losses, with several high-profile foreign brands shuttering their doors for good and leaving swathes of retail space vacant.

Data from the Urban Redevelopment Authority (URA) reveals that vacant retail space increased islandwide, from about 3.4 million sqft in early 2011 to 5.0 million sqft today.

The situation is similarly grim in Singapore's preeminent retail belt: Orchard Road. Vacant retail space hit a high of 700,000 sqft, representing 9.3% of the total lettable area, in 2Q2016. While official data shows that vacant space dropped to 550,000 sqft in 1Q2017, a walk through several malls reveals that the reduced vacancy is propped up by temporary "pop-up" stores that have blossomed like flowers in springtime. A shrinking jobs market, flat wage growth and a reduction of high rollers gaming in Singapore have a negative multiplier effect on the consumption levels of the luxury goods and services that are predominantly offered at Orchard Road.

Figure 1: Year-on-year growth for the monthly retail sales index (at current prices, excluding motor vehicles) seems to indicate a shrinking retail market as 27 of the last 39 months showed declines. Data as of March 2017.

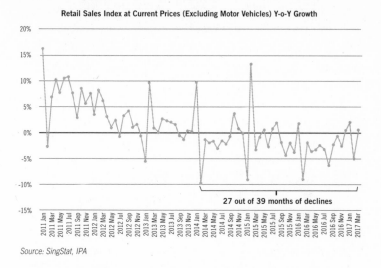

Retail Sales Index at Current Prices (Excluding Motor Vehicles) Y-o-Y Growth

27 out of 39 months of declines

Source: SingStat, IPA

Figure 2: Vacant lettable space and vacancy rate of retail malls in the Orchard Planning Area trended up until mid-2016 and then fell again when temporary "pop-up" stores started to occupy vacant shop lots in several malls.

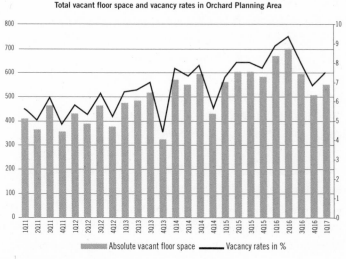

Total vacant floor space and vacancy rates in Orchard Planning Area

Absolute vacant floor space ——— Vacancy rates in %

Source: URA, IPA

The poor retail performance of Orchard Road sparked calls from a high-level government committee, the Committee on the Future Economy (CFE), to improve the situation. The Committee recommended that "the private sector partner the Government to embark on bold moves to transform Orchard Road into a vibrant shopping and lifestyle destination with a signature street experience in a city garden."

In addition, many opinion pieces, analyst reports and discussions over forum pages and social media offered suggestions on how Orchard Road might be transformed.

Top 5 suggestions to transform Orchard Road

1 Pedestrianise Orchard Road
2 Conduct more street-level activities with cultural events, performances, shows, festivals, exhibitions
3 Leverage technology to improve customer-retailer relationships and enhance shopper experience
4 Provide a wider range of brands, products and services
5 Increase the number of dining and entertainment options

The top suggestion put forth involved a fully pedestrianised Orchard Road, such that more fashion, cultural and arts activities and larger-scale street-level events can be held. Other popular suggestions recognised the need to embrace technology, such as indoor positioning systems, virtual and augmented reality, omnichannel touchpoints, etc. to improve retailer-customer interaction. Others urged retailers to provide a wider range of products, brands, services, dining and entertainment options.

However, no one addressed the root of the decline of Orchard Road: *consumers are not leaving their homes to shop.*

So what can a pedestrian-only street with a wider range of brands, products and F&B offerings do to help draw shoppers to Orchard Road? After all, most brands of products are available online and in the suburban malls. Our efficient delivery network also brings a wide range of cuisines straight to our dining tables at home.

What should we do with the abundant retail floor space in Orchard Road?

Let us unshackle ourselves from the concept of Orchard Road as a shopping district. We propose that Orchard Road be recreated with a new identity where shopping and F&B play supporting roles to personal services, namely: healthcare and education.

As a top priority, all existing area classified as retail could be given flexibility for a change of use to healthcare. Given the rapid increase in healthcare demand from the ageing mass affluent population in Singapore and in Asia, several malls in the Orchard Planning Area have already increased their floor area for healthcare services: Pacific Plaza, Lucky Plaza, Paragon, Wheelock Place and Shaw Centre. About 1.5 million sqft — or 20% of the total lettable area of Orchard Road retail space — could be pre-approved to accommodate a wide range of primary healthcare, such as specialist clinics, medical diagnostics, aesthetic clinics, traditional medicines, etc.; and allied healthcare, such as therapy and counselling, post-surgery rehabilitation services, nutrition consultants, physiology, etc.

The CFE could have noted that Singapore is not the only country facing an ageing population — most developed nations have greying populations — and the demand for healthcare services is sure to grow. The last available figure from the Singapore Tourism Board indicated that medical tourists spent almost S$1 billion in 2014 (STB stopped publishing the breakdown of medical tourism dollars for 2015 but instead categoried it under "Others" together with Business, Education, Airfare, Port Taxes, etc.).

Against the stiff competition for medical tourists from India, Malaysia and Thailand, the increasing vacant space in Orchard Road presents us with a great opportunity to build on Singapore's reputation for quality and safety in medical services, and transform Orchard Road into a one-stop destination for the full range of healthcare services.

To attract an even wider range of visitors to Orchard Road, we propose a second layer of services to be added: education.

There is global awakening in the need for lifelong learning and we propose that Orchard Road be positioned to offer a whole variety of education services. We envision another 20% of Orchard Road's 7.5 million sqft of retail space be filled with education services such as enrichment and music classes, tuition centres for students undertaking formal education, playschools for infants and children, skills training centres for working adults, private education centres with formal certificate programmes, experiential learning providers, multi-modal online-offline symposium facilities, etc. In fact, formal programmes involving retail, tourism, services and hospitality studies should cluster within Orchard Road as the learning experience is richer when learners are immersed in the industry.

Services such as speech and language therapy and occupational therapy straddle both the medical and education fields and their coexistence could establish Orchard Road as a centre for innovation in therapy practices, as well as skills training and education methodologies.

The other 60% of Orchard Road's net lettable area will continue to house retail shops, F&B outlets and other services such as hairdressers and tailors. These traditional services will complement and support the healthcare hub taking the primary role, and the education hub playing the secondary role in Orchard Road.

Conclusion

The retail paradise of today is in the cyberspace. The convenience of e-commerce gives consumers fewer reasons to visit physical stores. Brick-and-mortar retail space is fast becoming irrelevant in today's world; and hence, malls that primarily focused on attracting shoppers will go the way of the typewriter and the abacus.

It is time we shift our focus away from making Orchard Road a shopping district. Orchard Road needs to establish a new identity. Its retail space needs therapy. The medicine we prescribe is healthcare and education services.

Authors' Note

This article was not accepted for publication by several mainstream media. To make it even more puzzling, the editor of a media suggested that I remove the graphs and added that I might have missed out on attributing a government official's name to the idea of pedestrianizing Orchard Road. I decided to withdraw the submission.

A side note, as far back as 1995, the blueprints for pedestrianizing Orchard Road were drawn up. Both versions made Orchard a pedestrians-only street with one version having cars going underground and the other version with cars going over a viaduct.

PART 4

FROM AN INSIDER'S PERSPECTIVE

20. Hotspots: What's with All the Media Hype?

The article was co-authored with Janice Chin Li Ping and Shannon Aw Qian Tong, undergraduates from the Department of Real Estate, National University of Singapore.

1 August 2017, HugProperty.com

Over the past five years, dozens of articles published in mainstream media and property portals have variously labelled neighbourhoods all over Singapore as "hotspots" for investors to focus on. If we believed all the articles, we would consider almost the entire Singapore as a giant investment hotspot!

For an investor who has sufficient funds to place only one single bet, which is The Hottest Hotspot? Should we buy what these articles say and plunge in? Or should we do more homework and seek better advice from trustworthy agents?

Beyond the media articles, property portals and social media hype about investment hotspots are likewise plentiful and frequent. It just depends on the location of properties being marketed and how much online advertising budget marketers have.

What are the common justifications for these locations to be considered hotspots?

1. Proximity to MRT Stations and Bus Interchanges

In the context of residential properties, proximity to main transportation modes is a key criterion for most buyers. Thus, being

Figure 1: A sample of media articles highlighting investment hotspots for private residential districts around Singapore

Location	Date of publication	Weblink
Geylang	29 September 2012 17 January 2015	http://www.stproperty.sg/articles-property/singapore-property-news/geylang-a-growing-hot-spot-for-investors/a/87514 http://www.straitstimes.com/business/interactive-geylang-re-zoning-may-raise-condo-values
Yishun	4 October 2013 4 March 2013 26 February 2016	http://www.stproperty.sg/articles-property/hdb/a-new-mixed-development-in-yishun/a/138588 http://www.stproperty.sg/articles-property/financial-guide/yishun-up-and-coming-town/a/107835 http://brandinsider.asiaone.com/thewisteria/yishun-investment-hotspot/
Jurong	18 August 2014	http://www.straitstimes.com/singapore/6-reasons-jurong-will-be-a-truly-exciting-place
Botanic Gardens	14 August 2015	https://www.theedgeproperty.com.sg/content/property-hotspot-botanic-gardens
Outram Park	20 August 2015	https://www.theedgeproperty.com.sg/content/property-hotspot-pearl-bank-apartment
Paya Lebar	18 October 2016	http://www.straitstimes.com/business/property/paya-lebar-quarter-set-to-transform-area
Hougang	6 May 2016	http://brandinsider.straitstimes.com/starsofkovan/why-kovan-is-one-of-the-best-places-to-call-home/
District 9, 10, 11	12 February 2017	http://www.straitstimes.com/business/property/good-time-to-buy-that-dream-home
Woodlands	16 April 2017	http://www.straitstimes.com/singapore/housing/woodlands-to-transform-into-star-destination-of-the-north-with-new-housing

located near to Mass Rapid Transit (MRT) stations is a big selling point and property sellers will demand a premium if their properties are within minutes' walk to MRT stations.

Let us take a step back and reflect on this: does being close to an MRT station automatically make that residential neighbourhood an investment hotspot? Considering that one of the primary goals of the government is to make public transport the main mode of transportation and that the Land Transport Authority (LTA) has stated their objective that by 2030, 8 in 10 households will be living within 500 metres from an MRT station, will there still be a "MRT premium" by then?

There are also price maps comparing the average value of private properties around MRT stations across Singapore. A quick glance reveals that private residences within a few hundred metres of MRT stations in locations such as Pasir Ris and Choa Chu Kang can only achieve average prices below $900 per square foot (psf) while properties located within the same radius of MRT stations in the prime districts command average prices above $2,000psf.

Wow, what a surprise! The real hotspots for investors are still the prime districts!

By the year 2025, when another 50 MRT stations are added to the network, we believe that the premium of condominiums which are located near to MRT stations will almost disappear. However, the premium of a freehold property located in the prime districts will hold.

You may ask, what about the hype around Integrated Transport Hubs (ITH)? Apparently, being close to an ITH gives a residential property an added premium to those that are merely close to an MRT station or close to a bus interchange. We believe the same arguments apply:

- As more and more ITH's are built, the premium of condominiums around ITH's will be reduced.
- The perceived premium of ITH's may add pressure to the locations that are merely served by MRT stations only.
- The prime districts in Singapore will continue to hold a premium over mass market locations regardless of the proximity to MRT stations. In other words, a private apartment 1km away from the MRT in District 9 will have a higher value than a private apartment 100m away from the MRT in District 17.

2. Amenities and "Potential Redevelopment"

The classification of hotspots also includes "perks" in the neighbourhood, such as in the case of Hougang where an article

Probably the most recognisable street junction in Hougang, the junction of Simon Road and Upper Serangoon Road is in the Kovan neighbourhood, otherwise known as the "Lak Gor Jiok" or "sixth milestone area of Serangoon Road".

Photo by Ken Koh

touted it as "one of the best places to call home". The article highlighted that "nature lovers can easily escape to the rustic charms of Coney Island and Pulau Ubin". Hougang is not exactly within a five-minute bus ride to Pulau Ubin and it is only relatively nearer to Coney Island when compared to say, Jurong. In fact, you would have to drive through the towns of Sengkang and Punggol, change modes of transport at Punggol Point Jetty and loop back around the Punggol Promenade Nature Walk before you can reach the entrance of Coney Island. Sadly, the article leaves us with one conclusion: that it is scraping the bottom of the barrel in trying to glorify and elevate the Hougang precinct so that investors may pay attention to properties there.

There are other platforms that promote neighbourhood hotspots before any residential launch advertisements appear for that particular area. Property portals and discussion forums created by marketing agents frequently try to highlight the next gem to be unearthed. We urge investors to be careful and to distinguish whether the articles are written based on well-balanced research, or are hype-pieces written for marketing and promotional purposes.

In the Urban Redevelopment Authority (URA) Master Plan 2008, Paya Lebar Central was touted in the media as a regional commercial hub that will be an attractive, alternative location for businesses, bridging the distance between workplaces and homes. Riding on the promises of the Master Plan, the launch of Paya Lebar Square in 2012 was a success and the strata office units were snapped up in no time, supported by property investors who dived into the non-residential market to avoid the cooling measures imposed on residential investments.

At that time, marketing agents estimated that rentals could fetch $7psf per month, which would give investors gross rental yields of up to 4.5% against their purchase prices of as high as $2,000psf. Construction of Paya Lebar Square was completed in late 2014. As quoted in the *Straits Times* in April 2015, occupancy rates of the office units stood at 10%. About a year later in March 2016, *Straits Times* followed up on their story and found that only 50% of the office units are occupied. Half of Paya Lebar Square was vacant despite rents being adjusted lower, from the expected $7psf per month to $4psf per month, to attract more tenants. Investors were left with a lemony taste when market reality dashed the rosy forecasts made during the property launch.

Similarly, Geylang was introduced in an article in 2012 as a growing "hotspot for savvy property investors chasing high capital gains and rental yields" due to new residential launches, the Sports Hub in Kallang and the Paya Lebar regional financial centre. In January 2015, URA held a public consultation on their proposal to rezone parts of Geylang from residential-cum-institution use to a new commercial-cum-institution use.

Property experts immediately highlighted that reducing the space for homes will boost values for existing residences. They forecast that value will rise due to potential en bloc redevelopments as higher plot ratios may be assigned with the re-zoning. With attention focused on the redevelopment potential, instead of the usual attractions in Geylang such as food, amenities and proximity to the CBD, market punters speculated that Geylang is a hidden hotspot, overlooked due to its seedy image.

In fact, neighbourhood redevelopments, new Master Plans and dreams of increased plot ratios are common factors employed to hype up various locations as investment hotspots.

3. Master Plan and "Future Promises"

Jurong is touted by most people as a hotspot given that the Jurong Lake District has been designated to be Singapore's second CBD since the 2008 Master Plan. Adding to the euphoria of the High Speed Rail (HSR) terminus that will be built next to Jurong East MRT-cum-bus interchange are the big plans for Jurong Lake District, the grand designs for Jurong Innovation District and a brand new Tengah Forest Town that can house over 100,000 residents. Jurong is expected to be the hottest hotspot since Orchard Road!

Not that we are sceptical about the impressive makeover of Jurong, but here is the issue: are expectations running a decade ahead of reality? The announcement about the HSR has spawned many articles expressing the great potential value of residential properties in Jurong. In 2013 the authorities proclaimed an aggressive deadline: the HSR will be built by 2020. Investors, developers, property agents and their friends on social media all responded with a resounding "Invest now!"

Then in 2015, the year of completion was pushed back to 2022, and now, it is projected to be ready only in 2026. If investors had committed their money in residential properties in 2014 hoping for the game-changing element of the HSR to boost property values by 2020, would they feel a sense of regret today? Will there be further delays to the completion of the HSR? And why are property agents, analysts and the media still hyping up and speculating about the rise in property prices?

In fact, given the massive expectations about the certainty of rising property values in Jurong, we would caution investors to be extra careful about the "pent-up demand" there.

Conclusion

Most readers find it difficult to differentiate between genuine news articles and advertorials. Both online and in print, the layout of advertorials look similar to those of news articles. Worse, some online advertorials have web addresses that resemble those from mainstream media.

It is critical for investors to discern between well-balanced media articles and hype-articles that are sometimes masked as news. Investors should be mindful that these articles may have been sponsored by advertisers to market their products and perhaps written to boost the upcoming residential launches. So, be wary of what you read, online or offline. (Including this article!)

The end result of these articles is to give the impression that the entire Singapore private residential landscape is a giant hotspot. And ironically, the more hotspots there are, the longer the authorities will keep the cooling measures intact.

Now, back to our original question: for the investor who is keen to make one single property investment, which hotspot should he invest in? HugProperty recommends investors to invest time and effort in sourcing and appointing a trustworthy agent to provide unbiased advice.

ANALYSING
COMMON HOTSPOT CLAIMS
IN SINGAPORE'S
PROPERTY SCENE

In recent years, an increasing number of neighbourhoods are labelled as property hotspots for investment. Several claims were made to justify this **hotspot** title.

HOW TRUE ARE THESE CLAIMS?

WHAT THE CLAIMS CONSIDER AS A HOTSPOT

If a neighbourhood is accessible and has **plenty of public transport modes nearby**

If a neighbourhood has numerous amenities around

If a neighbourhood is **part of a Master Plan**, with future plans involved

FACTS:

By 2030, LTA projects that 8 in 10 households will be located within 500m of an MRT station, thus diminishing the advantage that accessibility provides.

Price maps show that prime districts will still beat out accessible neighbourhoods as hotspots.

Hougang was touted to be near Coney Island, but this proximity was revealed to be over-hyped by the media.

Plans are subject to changes and investors should be cautious of any unforeseen circumstances.

In 2013, Jurong Lake District was designated as the second CBD due for completion in 2020, prompting many investments in the area. But the completion was delayed continuously, dismaying the investors who took the plunge early.

CONCLUSION:

Investors must **exercise discretion** when choosing property hotspots to invest in.

Source: HugProperty.com

21. The Big Singapore Market Upgrade?

The article was co-authored with Shannon Aw Qian Tong, an undergraduate from the Department of Real Estate, National University of Singapore.

September 2017, HugProperty.com

Positive news in the real estate sector started to stream in early in 2017. We began the year with promising data from the manufacturing sector. The value of imports and exports also rose. Several new properties geared up for launches supported by the efforts of a few thousand agents distributing flyers, sending emailers, knocking on the doors of prospective investors and staging road shows all over Singapore. Developers with leftover units in a few dozen projects around Singapore also rode on the media and marketing hype.

Adding to the extensive market outreach of the property agents, real estate and financial analysts weighed in by proclaiming that residential market prices have already reached a bottom and will rise in 2017.

Are we really at the bottom? Are prices going to move up? Some market watchers point out that after 15 consecutive quarters of price declines, surely the market has to turn up!

Amongst the most bullish proclamations was a 60-page report by a leading global institution titled *Property Prices Inflecting and On Track to Double by 2030*. Published on 12 April 2017, mainstream media hungry for positive news immediately highlighted the key points: we are at the end of a protracted downtrend since 2013, property prices will rise from 2018, prices will sustain a 5% increase in dollar per square foot terms every year such that by 2030, the average values of private residences will double!

Market watchers, commentators, property agents and investors discussed the report in online forums and over social media. Several opined that in order for prices to double by 2030, Singapore would need more immigrants to hit a population of at least 7 million, or even limit new housing supply to market. A few also wondered about the wider implications of a doubling of housing prices.

We liked that the report is packed full of justifications about how strongly the Singapore economy will grow, and how that will push up housing prices. However, in trying so hard to stretch our imaginations about economic growth and home price growth, several justifications in the report seem to tread on the fringe of the debatable and dubious.

We have over a dozen questions about various areas of the report. In this piece, we would like to highlight the areas where the authors' arguments could be based on stronger foundations.

The report claimed that property prices will double by 2030 if all major economic and demographic factors are aligned. Three key points which contribute to the doubling of prices are: 1) the shrinking home sizes, 2) the Gross Domestic Product (GDP) and income growth, and 3) the household formation rate of singles and high-skilled Employment Pass holders.

Key Point 1 from the report:
Average unit sizes of private residential units sold by developers fell from 1.3k sqft to 1.1k sqft between 1995 to 2016, while the average size of five-room public housing units has fallen from 123sqm to 110 sqm since 1997. We believe home sizes will continue to decline at a rate of 1% per annum.

This argument assumes that a decrease in home sizes will lead to an increase in the price per sqft. Due to the generous dollops of cooling measures imposed on the residential market since 2009, developers have squeezed home sizes to keep the investment quantum low and to improve affordability for investors. This has resulted in brisk home sales for studio-sized, one-bedroom and two-bedroom units which are mainly purchased by investors who think that they can subsequently rent to low-budget tenants.

Our questions: Why does the report only consider the sizes of apartments sold by developers and conclude that "home sizes will continue to decline at the rate of 1% p.a."? In the event that developers only launched and sold apartments of 800sqft in the year 2018, would the report then infer that average home sizes would decline at an even faster rate of say, 5% per year? What about resale transactions? Older properties which are larger in size are more often purchased by families for their own use, and these are less frequently transacted than investors' units which are, on average, smaller in size.

Fact 1: The average size of Singapore's private homes did not reduce steadily from 1,300 sqft in 1995 to 1,100 sqft in 2016. The report charted data of developers' new sales only. For new sales, large sized apartments and penthouses were the rage in 2006–2008 and therefore average home sizes transacted in that period climbed above 1,500 sqft in early 2007. Sizes of new homes sold do not represent the sizes of all private homes in Singapore. Private homes include landed properties. However there were few new landed housing projects launched in the last 10 years as compared to compact apartments in high-density developments and the latter contributed to the shrinking sizes of new homes. Do note that new home sales account for about 10,000–12,000 units per year in the past 10 years but the total stock of private homes reached 348,000 by the end of 2016. Therefore, the smaller average sizes of 10,000 new homes every year hardly weigh down the average size the entire stock of private homes.

Fact 2: The sizes of new HDB flats have remained constant since 1997. HDB made a switch to reduce flat sizes in 1997 and since then, the average sizes of all new three-room, four-room and five-room flats have been maintained. Our gradually shrinking household sizes caused by a falling birth-rate has made HDB build a larger proportion of three-room and four-room flats. To cater for the needs of retirees and singles, HDB has also increased the number of studio and two-room flats in the past few years. As a result, the proportion of five-room flats has become smaller. The report claimed that "the average size of five-room public housing units has fallen from 123sqm to 110sqm since 1997". And it followed with the statement "we believe home sizes will continue to decline at the rate of 1% p.a." Uninformed readers may form an incorrect impression that HDB will reduce the sizes of new flats at a rate of 1% p.a. in future!

Certain data trends are not suitable for extrapolation. Would it be reasonable to extrapolate the world record times for a 100m sprint down to 3 seconds? Would it be reasonable to think that the average Singaporean will live in homes that measure 600 sqft in 50 years' time? Would this imply that about 50% of Singaporeans live in homes that are 200–600 sqft?

We find it puzzling that the report concluded that Singapore's average residential sizes will shrink by 1% p.a. from 2017–2030 simply based on historical trends of the sizes of new private home sold in the last 20 years and a groundless suggestion that HDB will reduce flat sizes in the next 14 years simply due to one reference data point from 1997.

Key Point 2:
Medium-term potential GDP growth for Singapore at 3.0% per annum over 2016–2030. Income growth of 4.0% per annum.

A doubling of dollar per sqft prices in the residential market from 2016–2030 implies an average of 5% per annum increase in prices. To make up the 5% growth, the authors "believe Singapore can achieve 4% growth in nominal GDP per capita over the long term based on 5% nominal GDP growth and 1% population growth". The 4% "per capita GDP growth" or income growth of the population implies that housing affordability will improve by 4% per year. Coupled with a 1% per annum decrease in the average sizes of homes, it means that a 5% dollar per sqft price growth per year is sustainable. The 5% nominal GDP growth assumption came with a "1.5–2.0% medium-term headline inflation". (Reference is made to page 27 of the report.)

Our question: Does a 10% income growth mean that a household will be able to afford to buy homes that cost 10% more? Housing affordability for renters could increase in tandem with income growth, that is, if wages increased by 10% a tenant could increase his rental budget by 10% to rent a bigger home or a home in a better location. But for home ownership, the correlation is debatable.

While each working household may achieve a consistent 4% per annum income growth, they still need to deal with inflationary pressures of 1.5–2.0% per annum and may not be able to afford homes which are getting pricier by 4% every year.

Flipping the question around, we ask if income growth and improved affordability will necessarily mean that housing prices will increase? In a market that is oversupplied with homes, with 31,000 vacant private residences and Executive Condominium units at the end of 1Q2017, and with rentals continuing to slide, income growth will not necessarily lead to home price growth.

Fact 3: The correlation between income growth and home price growth was negative, at least for 2016 anyway. Singapore's median household income in 2016 increased by 2.6% over 2015. However, over the same period, private residential rentals dropped 4.0% and private home prices dropped 3.1%. Income growth does not necessarily translate to home price growth. Not when we are in a multi-year oversupply situation.

Fact 4: A key contributor of the 2.6% household income growth in 2016 is a 15% increase in households with *zero income*. Figure 1 below shows that in 2016, the proportion of households with income from work grew by 1.8% over 2015 while the proportion of households with *no working persons* increased by 15%! The shrinking employment market in the past two years were mainly attributed to the lower income jobs in sectors such as offshore and marine, oil and gas, construction and retail services. When the lower income households fall into zero income, the remaining families with stable income will lift the nationwide average income. We recognise that there are families whose household incomes have indeed risen and that Singapore continues to accept new Permanent Residents and new citizens who have high income. Therefore we are not attributing the entire 2.6% income growth to the large 15% increase in households which have stopped earning. We simply want readers to be mindful about how statistics may be reported.

Figure 1: Increase in total number of resident households, compared to households with at least one working person and no working persons.

	2015 (in thousands)	2016 (in thousands)	Increase in number of households between 2016 and 2015 (in thousands)	Increase in number of households by percentage
Number of resident households	1,225.3	1,263.6	38.3	3.1%
Households with at least 1 working person (resident employed households)	1,106.5	1,126.9	20.4	1.8%
Households with no working persons	118.8	136.6	17.8	15.0%
(Retiree households)	81.2	94.7	13.5	16.6%

Notes:

a) A resident household refers to a household headed by a Singapore citizen or Permanent Resident.

b) For statistical purposes, "retiree households" are defined as those comprising solely non-working persons aged 60 years and over. "Retiree households" are included in the category of "households with no working persons".

Source: SingStat, IPA

In view of the large increase in households without income, the 2.6% household income growth in 2016 is nothing to celebrate about. It is akin to a school reporting an improvement in students' average grades from B to B+ simply by sacking all the students with C and D grades. Will the school stage a celebration for that?

Fact 5: GDP growth amidst employment decline will be the new normal. To top off this discussion, the first quarter 2017 GDP growth came in at 2.7% against: a) an overall reduction of 6,800 jobs, b) a 0.9% decline in residential rentals and c) a 0.4% decline in private home prices. Since mid-2013, Singapore has experienced steady GDP growth amidst 15 continuous quarters of home price declines. The report scarcely considered the large number of vacant homes and oversupply of housing stock that are depressing the market even while economic growth stayed positive. The total number of jobs and employment opportunities will impact the population growth and taken together, those indicators are more meaningfully correlated to housing demand than the actual value of our GDP.

The report further stated that historically, a 7% per annum dollar per sqft price growth was achieved in the period of 1975 to 2016 and therefore, "we believe home prices will double by 2030 and offer an average 5% in annual appreciation per year. We believe a 5% long-term growth rate will keep pace with income growth, keeping affordability levels (as measured by home price to income) stable."

Our questions are simple: is it reasonable to use historical growth to justify forward growth? Are the economic factors and policy levers available in the last 40 years still available in the next 14 years?

The 7% per annum growth over the period of 1975 to 2016 started from a very low base. The private residential price index, normalised at 100 points in 1Q2009, was a mere 10 points in 1975 and 137 points at the end of 2016. Growing 7% per annum from a base of 10 index points is probably a little easier to achieve than growing 5% per annum from a base of 137 index points.

Over those 40 years, population growth was rapid, from about 2.2 million to 5.6 million, with high annual growth rates achieved in several years such as 4.8% in 1981, 4.2% in 1996, 4.3% in 2007 and 5.5% in 2008. That growth boosted the demand for housing and, over a smaller base of residential stock, that demand translated into price growth.

Several other factors added to the increase of home prices in the past decades:

- the strong government push for home ownership which, in our best estimates drawn from HDB reports, rose from below 50% in 1975 to 90% in 2016,
- the accumulation of CPF monies in the earlier years and a subsequent relaxation of rules around the use of CPF for purchasing homes,
- increased plot ratios for housing developments and higher quality homes built with better material and specifications, both contributed to home values, and
- a young workforce in the 1980s to 2010s (comprising of the baby boomers) with increasingly better education, the majority of whom are employed by multi-national companies and a growing public service with attractive salaries.

Fact 6: Population growth will be low, at 1.5% per annum. Looking forward, in the period of 2017 to 2030, assuming that we can achieve the population target of 6.9 million in 2030, the annual population growth rate will average at 1.5%. This growth is strongly premised on the ability to create jobs while sustaining GDP growth at between 2–4% per annum till 2030. However, as discussed in the paragraphs above, Singapore achieved positive GDP growth amidst a decline in employment in 1Q2017. The future of jobs creation is a question mark given the rapid advancement of robotics, more powerful software and new technology. In the next 10 years, it is conceivable that redundancies will outpace new jobs even while GDP grows. So where will demand for residential properties come from? Not robots for sure!

Fact 7: Home ownership has hit a peak. Home ownership has hovered around 90% for the last 20 years and no matter despite policy makers' push for 100% home ownership, there will be families who are not able to, or choose not to, own their homes. If we are not able to create sufficient jobs to bring about an increase of foreign workers, there are only two ways to increase home purchases: splitting household units and getting more investors to buy (but will they buy knowing that rentals are not looking up?).

Fact 8: There are few policy levers that can mitigate old age and death. Our population is aging and the workforce is no longer young. The number of "retiree households" increased from 54,000 in 2008 to 95,000 in 2016, a 76% increase over 8 years. The size of this group will only increase further: in the 10 year period from 2017 to 2026, about 558,000 Singaporean baby boomers will cross into retirement age of 60 (based on Department of Statistics' definition in tabulating household incomes). In contrast, only 461,000 young Singaporeans will "graduate" past the average first-time home-buying age of 25.

Whilst we agree that there will be new home sales and new family formation, we have to be mindful that many retirees also need to cash out of their homes for retirement. Further, we need to note that the total number of deaths due to old age will increase over the next 15 years as the 1 million baby boomers (who are between 51–69 years of age today) approach the median life expectancy of about 85 years.

Key Point 3:
The increase in single-person households will drive up the demand for housing.

The report stated that the "growing number of single person households — which comprised one in eight Singapore resident households in 2010 — has been a key contributor to housing demand. Given rising singlehood rates, we forecast that by 2030, one in five households will be occupied by just one person."

The authors further estimated that the number of single-person households will increase from 139,800 (which makes up 12% of total households) in 2010, to 218,500 in 2020 (16% of total households) and 297,300 in 2030 (19% of total households). The rate of increase in resident households will outpace the slow population growth, becoming a key demand driver for small, shoebox-sized homes in Singapore.

Our questions: What are the reasons behind the increase in single-person households? What is the proportion of single-person households that are young, economically active singles who chose to live alone, versus singles who may be widowed or divorced?

Fact 9: The increased number of single-person households, about 78,800 over the 10 year period of 2020 to 2030, may not translate into significant demand for private properties.

Firstly, a big contributor to the growing number of single-person households in the next 20 years will be widowed households. Our large aging population of baby boomers will start to pass on in greater numbers in about 10–15 years' time. The retired and surviving widower (for simplicity, let us assume that the word "widower" and "he" refer to both genders) would be classified under the household survey as an additional, single-person household. He would probably already have a home so there will be no net increase in housing demand. On the contrary, if he wishes to cash out of his home and move in with his children and grandchildren, there will be a net supply of one additional home on the market.

Secondly, looking at the young, say below 40, who chose singlehood, might the authors have considered that housing affordability may be halved for these single-person households? Compared to a couple buying a home, a single person will not have as much savings in cash and CPF for the down payment, and will be more limited in his ability to service loans. Therefore, if there is higher demand from people who chose singlehood, that demand would be skewed to the public housing segment rather than private homes.

Thirdly, a "resident household" is defined by SingStat and United Nations Statistics Division as: "a household headed by a Singapore citizen or permanent resident. A household refers to a group of two or more persons living together in the same house and sharing common food or other arrangements for essential living. It also includes a person living alone or a person living with others but having his own food arrangements. Although persons may be living in the same house, they may not be members of the same household." This simply means that four persons living under one roof could be comprised of three households: the father and mother as a household, and two adult working children who have their own food arrangements.

The facts above are not laid out to claim that there will not be additional demand for new private homes from single-person households. We are simply saying that within the report's estimated increase of 78,800 single-person households between 2020 and 2030, some of the additional single-person households may be actually be selling their homes (i.e. net negative demand), some may purchase private residences with their limited budget and most of them may go for HDB flats.

On a related note to the single-person owner-occupiers, the report further argues that the increase in the minimum salaries of Employment Pass (EP) holders will lead to higher demand for housing and there will be higher Internal Rate of Return (IRR) for residential investments. We think that the increase in the minimum wage of EP holders from $3,300 to $3,600 in January 2017 may improve the rental demand but not the buying of private properties. An EP holder will have to be earning at least $8,000 a month to be able to purchase a private housing unit in Singapore provided he has sufficient savings to make the down payment and the stamp duties. A $700,000 shoebox unit will require most EP holders to fork out about $400,000 for down payment, normal stamp duty and Additional Buyer Stamp Duty. In today's market, a $700,000 shoebox private residence in the outskirts of Singapore rents for about $1,800 per month. We believe that EP holders' will do their sums and will opt to rent. The increase in EP holders' minimum wage will NOT affect the private housing market.

There are many more points that we would like to highlight including:

- Claim: Household balance sheets are strong.

  We say: (a) The official data on household debt do not capture loans for cars and properties held under companies; (b) Mortgage rates has only one direction to go when the world exits from the long interest rates slumber.

- Claim: Unsold inventory is at an all-time low.

  We say: Official data on unsold inventory only reflects unsold apartments in projects which are still licensed by the Controller of Housing. Unsold stock in residential projects which have received the Certificate of Statutory Completion are dropped from the data set.

- Claim: Exhibits 49 and 55 of the report showed a constant 2% annual rental yield where rentals increase 5% per year as well as a 5% price appreciation per year from 2017 to 2030.

  We ask: Have the authors assumed that rental income is continuous over the 14-year period, without any vacancy periods between tenants? And we wonder if the economy will be recession-free throughout the entire period. If the economy were blazing hot, would the costs of property ownership rise significantly?

Conclusion

We are not convinced by the justifications behind the forecast that the average private residential prices in Singapore will rise to $2,000psf in 2030.

The current reality is that the private residential market continues to face tougher and tougher challenges such as ageing population, slower jobs growth and low birth rate. We are likely to see property prices dragging along on a protracted downturn for several more years before recovering.

We observe several dichotomies in the property market and these contradicting data-sets indicate that the recent exuberance and hype around new property launches, land sales and en bloc activities are not anchored on firm foundations.

Some of the opposing data-sets in the market are (as of writing this article in mid-July 2017):

- GDP growth is being revised upwards after a strong 1Q2017 but employment shrank by 6,800 positions in 1Q2017. We ask: which is more important to housing — employment or GDP?

- Exuberance in new property launches (mainly sales of one- and two-bedroom units imply that buyers are investors) but rentals keep dropping. We ask: if investors cannot find tenants, how long can this situation last?

- Researchers and analysts are calling market bottom now and upturn in 2017–2018, but yet these same companies' valuations departments and en bloc sales departments are giving low valuation estimates to sellers. We ask: are the property consultants internally undecided about the market direction?

- New sales are moving up but bank valuations of resale properties are not improving. We ask no questions about this.

- Real estate transaction volumes increase in the past few months but both the price index and rental index drop. This happens a lot in the stock markets, such as on Black Monday, where the volume of transactions are very high but prices crashed. We ask: should we celebrate Black Monday?

- The sharing economy will trend up over the next decade and home sharing may temper the demand for home ownership. We ask: should we promote new technologies for home sharing on one hand, while investing into physical real estate on another?

Our purpose of writing this article is to highlight to our readers that while positive headlines on Singapore real estate is always welcome, we often need to dive deeper into the figures to understand the full picture. Viewpoints will differ, and the wide range of opinions add to the colour and debate to make the Singapore real estate market a lively one. If the devil is in the details, then we ought to get to know the devil very well.

As market analysts and commentators, we seek to help readers understand find more meaning and relevance about the real estate market.

22. The Patterns of Dodgy Property Agents

The article was co-authored with Janice Chin Li Ping, an undergraduate from the Department of Real Estate, National University of Singapore.

15 August 2017, HugProperty.com

In today's competitive services market, real estate agents are not only caught in the strife of industry competition, they also have to grapple with being made redundant by technology. To say that there are many real estate agents in Singapore is an understatement — there are more than 28,000 licensed agents, or about one agent serving every 140 residents; and this is probably the principal cause of the stiff competition in the industry. The competition is exacerbated by the growing number of buyers, sellers, landlords and tenants who opt for self-service through web applications. We are concerned that some agents have compromised their integrity and their "duty of care" for their clients in order to trump the competition.

So, buyers, sellers, landlords and tenants: beware! We want to highlight to you that many of the listings on property portals and websites are not real. Those seemingly attractive and enticing deals may just be potholes for you to step into. We have encountered several of these unfortunate events ourselves, and in this article, we highlight some red flags that you should keep a lookout for. It is vital that you take precaution to ensure that you do not fall into the traps created by a few crafty agents.

Scenario A

Fake news and listings are increasingly common: The agent you call does not have an actual listing of the property you saw online.

A property listing is an advertisement of a property that is put up for sale or for lease. Listings may appear on property portals or in traditional print media, such as the classified ads in the newspapers. Sellers and landlords may appoint one or more licensed real estate agents to list the properties to attract buyers and tenants. Conversely, buyers and tenants may also engage real estate agents to source for suitable properties that meet their budgets and needs.

To think that all listings of properties are genuine and available at any point in time is to picture a world of sunshine and rainbows. The sad truth is: there are many cases of fake listings put up to bait direct buyers and tenants.

We term these fake listings "imitations". Why so? They look almost identical to other real listings, but upon careful inspection, something may be amiss. These imitations sometimes use photos or descriptive information copied from listed properties posted by other property agents. Sometimes, even after a property has been sold, unscrupulous agents might copy the property's photos for use in their fake listings. We have experienced several of such cases and we have highlighted these imitations to the owners of the apartments. These agents would quickly remove the imitations after the owners have called to inquire if the agents were given the permission to represent them for sale or for rent.

Usually, imitations use very attractively low prices to entice buyers and tenants because they look like "good deals that should not be missed". Then when direct clients call these agents to enquire, the usual responses are that the property is "sold" or "taken" or "no longer available", and the agents will immediately ask, "May I show you another apartment in the same block?" If the agent received calls from other property agents who are representing buyers, they either do not pick up the calls or they do not return calls. This is commonly seen in districts 9, 10 and 11 where transaction values are higher and the probability of attracting unsuspecting foreign buyers and tenants is likewise higher. Higher value properties also translate to a higher quantum of the 1% agent fees, which is sufficiently rewarding for the agents to put in efforts to pull such tricks.

We estimate that up to 20% of the listings posted online are not genuine. The percentage could be higher for luxury developments. Buyers who receive such replies from agents should immediately congratulate the agent that the property is already sold or leased out, and then hang up the phone. To avoid being further prospected by that agent, buyers would do well to appoint a trustworthy agent to do their home search. Let your agent represent you and let him sieve out and deal with the numerous imitations in the property portals.

Scenario B
The agent has actual properties to list, but the information is misleading.

Fake-lister agents deliberately post listings of properties with incredibly low prices to attract direct buyers and tenants. Unsuspecting buyers and tenants will then ring the agents up because they may reflect the lowest dollar per square foot price ($psf) or rental for that condominium unit. The $psf may give a different impression in different contexts. For example, if a buyer wishes to compare prices in the same district or perhaps properties with similar attributes but in different condominium blocks, $psf will be a key metric in measuring the relative value of the properties. Merely showing the buyers how cheap a property is based on $psf comparisons without describing much about the size and layout of the property does not reveal much about whether the property is really well-priced.

The buyer may see an advertisement for a 750 sqft apartment for sale at $980psf (i.e. $735,000) in a condominium where the average transacted prices in the last year were around $1,200psf. It gives the impression of a $220psf discount from the recent transacted average. However, only when the buyer views the apartment will he realise that the very "cheap" 750 sqft apartment is a shoebox unit with 450 sqft of built-in area, a 260 sqft patio and another 40 sqft air-conditioner ledge. Or it could be a "penthouse" unit with 400 sqft of built-in area, a 300 sqft roof terrace and a 50 sqft stairwell. The low $psf price is deliberately highlighted to create the impression that the property is a great buy. Buyers and tenants, do take note! Many other variations of the same pattern exist. Most times, information that is not revealed is more important than information that is highlighted.

While some agents withhold information, other agents offer a lot of information about the properties to show how knowledgeable they are about a particular condominium or district. They would purposely post many listings in a particular district they claim to be active in, to impress upon prospective buyers and tenants that they "specialise" in that neighbourhood. Unsuspecting clients may be dazzled by these agents, but tell-tale signs could be seen from their overenthusiasm. For example, in a listing for a condominium in Sentosa Cove, the agent included a description "near HarbourFront MRT Station". An agent who understands the needs of the residents in Sentosa Cove will not highlight the MRT station, and will certainly not say that HarbourFront Station is near.

While we would love to believe that some agents are really familiar with certain districts or market segments, we need to be mindful that many of them just want to create that impression so that they have a higher chance of being contacted by prospective clients.

We have merely touched on a handful of examples of the many patterns we have encountered. To discuss all the cases we regularly see will require too many pages. The ultimate aim of these agents is simple: to cut out other agents in order to get direct clients to call them, to swing these clients to their own actual listings or to get the clients to appoint them as a buyer's representative. Unfortunately, in trying to outwit the competition, they create misinformation in the market.

In the speech on Budget 2017, the Minister of State for National Development Dr Koh Poh Koon spoke about how "it may be more important for property agents now to hone their skills in servicing clients and building up their credentials rather than just competing on marketing and closing transactions." We wish that more agents will adopt this attitude and compete on service, rather than conjuring smoke and mirrors.

We are deeply concerned about the clients' interest and we wrote this piece to raise awareness about the patterns displayed by dodgy agents to fend off competition. We recommend clients to carefully select an agent that they feel comfortable with and to appoint the agent exclusively to represent them, whether it is for a property search (for purchase or rent), or to list a property (for sale or let). The appointed agent will be fully motivated to represent the clients' best interests and diligently assist clients in marketing or searching for properties.

More importantly, your exclusive agent will be able to ward off the dodgy agents with colourful patterns.

Author's Note

While we were researching and preparing this article, the Council for Estate Agencies published a disciplinary case in their 02/2017 newsletter titled *Cost of Misleading and False Ads — $17,500*. The CEA highlighted several cautionary points arising from the errant property agent's actions: placing fake or dummy advertisements, placing advertisements without property owners' consent and omitting mandatory details in advertisements. Readers who are keen to know more about the case may refer to the online newsletter here: https://www.cea.gov.sg/docs/default-source/module/newsletter/2-2017/website/cost-of-misleading-and-false-ads.html

Exposing the patterns of dodgy property agents

With about **1 agent for every 140 residents,** the stiff competition has driven some agents to compromise on their integrity so as to attract direct clients.

Two patterns commonly displayed by agents fishing for direct clients

Scenario A

Fake Listings

⚠️ Agent has no actual listing of the property but is posting up information copied from other listings.

We estimate that **up to 20% of the listings posted online are fake**

 Tell-tale signs of fake listings:

Pricing is too good to be true

Recommends another unit after informing property has been sold.

👍 What to do in this scenario:

Congratulate the agent on his sale and hang up to avoid being prospected.

Appoint trustworthy agents for your home search, let them filter out the unruly agents.

Scenario B

Misleading Information

🔒 Withholding / omitting information

Puts low $psf* price and excludes important details

Eg. A **750sqft unit** with a low $psf price **turns out to be 450 sqft of living space** with a 260 sqft patio and a 40 sqft air-con ledge

*Dollar Per Square Foot

📢 Excessive information

Purposely posts multiple listings in the district to **pose as a specialist** of that district

 Tell-tale signs of fake specialists

Unfamiliar with the development or district posted

Eg. A Sentosa Cove condo listing claims to be "near to Harbourfront MRT Station" – **which is inaccurate information.**

Source: HugProperty.com

23. Self-Service Potholes

The article was co-authored with Janice Chin Li Ping, an undergraduate from the Department of Real Estate, National University of Singapore.

September 2017, HugProperty.com

Self-service property websites lure property buyers, sellers, landlords and tenants (let us collectively address them as "Clients") with the bait of substantial savings in agents' fees. The proliferation of self-service portals and mobile applications has resulted in an increasing number of Clients who help themselves in transacting properties, particularly those who have more time and are a bit more tech- and legal-savvy. The results are apparently rather positive in the more price-sensitive HDB segment, where it is claimed that approximately one in four transactions in early 2016 were concluded without an agent representing either the buyer, or the seller.

Such publicity in the media inspires more Clients to go down the path of self-service, only for many to trip into potholes in the midst of their property transactions. Those botched transactions have generally gone unreported as the cases are somewhat embarrassing for Clients to admit. Some negative examples could have been ignored because such stories do not go well in this age of technology and skills upgrading.

As property agents who are familiar with the intricacies of rentals and investment transactions, we are saddened to find out that most of these issues could have been avoided if professional advice were sought from the beginning. Below are the common pitfalls that Clients face when they self-serve.

Buyers

A negative sale takes place when the transacted price is below the outstanding bank loan of the seller. For example, a buyer is attracted by a property which the seller has purchased for $4.0 million during the 2007 peak and is now available at a bargain price of $2.8 million. However, the property has an outstanding bank loan of $3.0 million and the bank will need to recover $200,000 from the seller before the bank releases the caveat to the buyer. With no prior knowledge of the seller's background, and in a rush to secure the seemingly attractive deal, this self-service buyer quickly hands over a cheque of $28,000 (i.e. the option money which is 1% of the $2.8 million price). The seller banks in the cheque. If bankruptcy charges were brought upon the seller by his creditors, the end point of this transaction will be a failure to grab the attractively priced property and a potential loss of $28,000 for the buyer.

However, if the buyer had appointed an agent, the situation could be different. Based on the large drop from the $4.0 million purchase price to the $2.8 million selling price, any agent worth their salt would do a thorough check on the seller's financial position. To reduce the risks that the buyer would face, the agent could recommend that the 1% option money be held by the buyer's appointed lawyer. No one should purchase a property without first checking if the seller, or one of the named owners, is fighting a case of bankruptcy.

Furthermore, buyers purchasing properties also face substantial difficulty trying to look into the background and the condition of the properties due to "information asymmetry". Not all properties are constructed to the same standards, and some have a reputation for having cut corners during construction. Investors and buyers who self-serve will not get the good counsel from experienced agents and industry players who would have heard the whispers (for example, of defects or the use of inferior materials).

A note about fees for agents: The current general industry practice is for the seller's agent to receive a success fee from the seller upon the closing of the transaction. The seller's agent then shares the fee with the buyer's agent, if any. We would like to propose another approach for buyers to consider: Buyers could appoint a "buyer's representative agent" and offer to pay the agent a success fee too. Given that this will be a novel practice, we are certain that it will be a great motivator for the agent to represent the buyer's best interests instead of being compromised on the fee sharing arrangement when negotiating with the seller's agent.

Sellers

When divesting their properties, sellers who opt for self-service may face a whole lot of challenges too.

Marketing a property is not as easy as just posting a "property for sale" up on the various property websites and waiting for calls from buyers or buyers' agents. It involves setting a reasonable asking price, screening the calls for genuine cases, arranging viewings and negotiating the sale.

Setting a reasonable price is critical because if the property is priced appropriately from the start, the seller will be able to attract genuine prospective buyers who have that budget, such that the property can be sold within a reasonable time on the market. On the other hand, if the property is priced at a premium in anticipation of hard bargaining, it deters prospective buyers and buyers' agents from making enquiries. Not only will the property be listed for a considerably longer time, it will simply be assisting other lower-priced listings to sell as buyers are motivated to call the low-priced listings first. However, if a seller engaged a property agent with rich experience, the agent will advise the optimal asking price and a target closing price, potentially leading to a smoother and faster transaction.

Secondly, there is the viewings and negotiation process to consider. DIY sellers will have to manage enquiries and negotiations with the buyers or buyers' agents on their own. Are these sellers ready to handle the enquiries? Some calls are merely for market comparison while others may result in viewing appointments. Having an appointed agent will simplify the screening of enquiries, the arrangement of viewings and the discussion of the terms of sale because the agent will represent sellers' best interests and diligently assist in negotiating for the ideal price.

Finally, when a reasonable offer has been accepted, sellers may want to take caution especially in granting the Option to Purchase (OTP) to the buyers. The buyer and his agent may have requested for variation to the terms of the OTP or stipulated certain conditions regarding the final handover of the property. A DIY seller is not likely to be experienced enough to handle the closing process and the paperwork required. Every term in the contract has to be properly considered to avoid legal consequences and other inconveniences relating to the handover of the property.

Landlords and Tenants

In Singapore, dual representation under the Council for Estate Agencies' regulation is not allowed. This means that a property agent should not represent both the landlord and the tenant who are in a leasing transaction.

A landlord's agent assists the landlord to list the property for rent and to check the eligibility of the prospective tenant. This is especially important since most tenants are foreigners holding work passes. If the tenant stays beyond the expiry of the work pass, the landlord can be charged with harbouring an illegal immigrant. A landlord's agent will verify the tenant's passes with the relevant authorities and ensure that the tenancy agreement is in line with the expiry dates of the passes. A good agent will also check on the prospective tenant's ability to pay rent on the agreed schedule as stated in the tenancy agreement.

On the other hand, a tenant's agent assists a tenant in sourcing for the most comfortable home to live in. A good agent will also highlight the properties that the tenant should avoid and perform background checks to verify that the landlord has the authority to let out the property on behalf of all the named owners.

Both the landlord's agent and the tenant's agent will negotiate and settle on a reasonable set of conditions in the tenancy agreement with appropriate terms that are in line with standard market practices. The tenancy agreement is a critical document for both the parties as it represents their respective rights to the property.

Should either one party or both decide to DIY, they should be mindful of several possible areas of friction that may arise, such as:

- Advanced termination of lease,
- Delayed rental payment, or non-payment,
- Damage or wear-and-tear to the property during tenancy,
- And, in the case of room rentals, what happens if tenant and landlord are not able to live amicably under the same roof?

In any of the above cases where either one of the parties deviates from the contract, it is difficult for the unrepresented party to assert his rights because the DIY contract may not have sufficiently covered that party's interests. However, if both landlord and tenant are represented by agents, each of the appointed agents can play the role of an advisor or a mediator to bridge the differences between the landlord and the tenant.

Conclusion

In a nutshell, saving on agent fees today may mean more expenses in future due to unforeseen circumstances and potential disputes. A good property agent will help to smooth out the many kinks that arise in the buy, sell or lease transaction, managing the buyer-seller negotiations and the landlord-tenant relationships. We believe that Clients who spend a little on agents' fees now will stand to save more in future.

New technological platforms may tease the potential for market disruption and the cutting out of middlemen, seducing Clients into thinking that they can self-serve to save money. However, we believe that self-help should be reserved for the accredited and savvy property investors. We urge Clients to be mindful about falling into potholes scattered on the DIY roads and instead seek professional assistance.

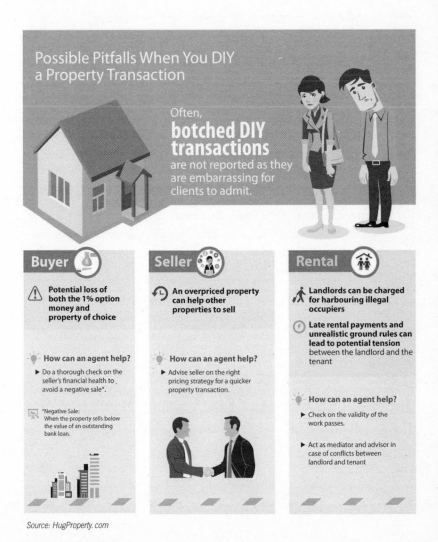

Possible Pitfalls When You DIY a Property Transaction

Often, **botched DIY transactions** are not reported as they are embarrassing for clients to admit.

Buyer

⚠ Potential loss of both the 1% option money and property of choice

💡 **How can an agent help?**

▶ Do a thorough check on the seller's financial health to avoid a negative sale*.

*Negative Sale: When the property sells below the value of an outstanding bank loan.

Seller

An overpriced property can help other properties to sell

💡 **How can an agent help?**

▶ Advise seller on the right pricing strategy for a quicker property transaction.

Rental

Landlords can be charged for harbouring illegal occupiers

Late rental payments and unrealistic ground rules can lead to potential tension between the landlord and the tenant

💡 **How can an agent help?**

▶ Check on the validity of the work passes.

▶ Act as mediator and advisor in case of conflicts between landlord and tenant

Source: HugProperty.com

24. Should I Set up a Company to Buy Singapore Property?

The article was co-authored with Goh Bun Hiong, an accredited tax advisor with PKF-CAP Advisory Partners Pte Ltd.

28 October 2016, TODAY

A substantial part of my work as a property agent involves representing sophisticated investors who are supported by their investment advisors, such as private bankers and accountants. With these investors, we are occasionally asked for opinions about whether they should set up Special Purpose Companies (SPCs) to invest in Singapore properties.

I learnt from my clients that they see several advantages for setting up an SPC to hold a Singapore property:

- Inheritance and wealth transfer. While there are no advantages in terms of savings on inheritance taxes in Singapore, a high net worth individual who is senior in age may invest in properties under an investment trust, a family foundation or an offshore vehicle to facilitate the ease of wealth distribution and transfer to selected beneficiaries and loved ones.

- Owning a residential property through an SPC attracts a 15% Additional Buyer Stamp Duty (ABSD). However, at the point of divesting the property, should the next buyer opt to buy over the shares of the SPC, the next buyer will save a significant sum on stamp duties. Depending on the jurisdiction where the SPC has been set up (e.g. the Cayman Islands or the British Virgin Islands), the stamp duties on the transfer of shares could be zero. If the shares of the company were sold within four years, the seller is not liable for Seller's Stamp Duty.

- Buying a non-residential Singapore property through an SPC is even more common as there is no deterrent in the form of the hefty 15% ABSD. Especially for larger assets, such as an office for the investor's use, it is an opportunity to minimise Goods and Services Tax (GST). This could yield significant savings.

- Having an SPC own the property separates the property ownership, income and expenses from the high net worth investor's personal income, which may bring advantages and savings in personal income tax.

However, owning a property under an SPC requires more upfront planning, effort and costs. There could also be disadvantages in the restrictions on home loans. In cases where SPC shares are transferred for the sole purpose of selling a property, the tax authorities may also assess if the set-up of the SPC was for the avoidance of real estate stamp duty and taxes.

We can look at this from another angle. An investor asked, "I'm considering buying an apartment as my home, and it seems that the seller owns the apartment under an SPC. The seller suggested that I buy over the shares of the company instead of buying the property directly. This will reduce my stamp duty to just 0.2% of the transaction value, meaning I will get to save on the Buyer Stamp Duty and the ABSD. What are your views on the seller's suggestion?"

My Answer

One needs to be aware of the possibility of the IRAS "looking through" the SPC structure to determine if its sole aim was for the purpose of aggressive tax reduction. In addition, for an overseas SPC, the ongoing yield of the overseas SPC could be significantly reduced by:

- Withholding taxes which could be applied against the rental income to the SPC
- Dividend distributions by the SPC which may not qualify as tax exempt income
- Income of the SPC which may be brought to tax by one or more tax jurisdictions, depending on the specific residency situation of the investor

Should you decide to proceed, you should also note that the purchase procedure will be different from a normal one: instead of receiving a standard Option to Purchase, you may receive a letter of offer for the sale of the SPC's shares.

Thereafter, you would need to engage the services of an experienced lawyer and accountant to look through the corporate background of the SPC and its financial accounts. Your lawyer and accountant will provide their opinions about whether the SPC and its accounts have any outstanding liabilities and obligations, and they will give their opinions about the risks of investing in the shares of the SPC.

SPC-held properties also have additional restrictions with regards to financing. For example, under the current Total Debt Servicing Ratio (TDSR) rules, the maximum loan-to-value ratio for a residential property held under an SPC is 20%. But if you are buying in cash, this is not a concern.

Another complication with loans: when you decide to sell the property in future, the next buyer of the SPC may not be able to take over the mortgage under this SPC. He would likely have to buy over the SPC in full cash, such that the existing mortgage is discharged and then take on a fresh mortgage when the SPC ownership is completely transferred. At that point, the SPC would have several years of accounts and history, and so the next buyer's financial due diligence process might take longer and cost more.

Other points to note include the compliance checks, anti-money laundering checks and the entire due diligence process. These could get complicated, especially for overseas SPCs and foreign bank accounts. There are also annual corporate secretarial and accounting costs in maintaining the SPC.

All things considered, the higher level of complexity including the additional efforts — and expenses involved — are usually more than compensated in terms of tax savings for the institutional investors and high net worth investors, where large assets such as commercial buildings, retail malls or factories are involved. The proliferation of shoebox retail, industrial and commercial properties in the last five years saw many individual owners purchasing such properties under Singapore registered companies. However, the benefits for an individual investor setting up an SPC to own a small strata-titled property of say, below S$2 million, is not so clear cut.

In my reply to the investor, I had to add a caveat that as a real estate agent, I am licensed to advise on property transactions but I am not qualified to provide tax opinions. Investors should consult experienced lawyers and tax accountants for detailed assessments about their financial circumstances.

PART 5

VENTURING
FURTHER AFIELD

25. Ganbatte Japan!

The article was co-authored with Huang Shi Hui, an undergraduate from the Department of Real Estate, National University of Singapore.

Japan's real estate market is slowly and surely trending up. Prices and rentals have been creeping up ever since Mr Shinzo Abe took office as Prime Minister in late 2012. His economic policies have given Japan's stagnant economy a boost, and that has created jobs which, in turn, has lifted demand for properties. One of the property segments with good investment opportunity is the residential segment, especially in the key cities. There are two good reasons why. Firstly, the rental returns are higher compared to developed countries like Singapore. Secondly, Japan's previously closed economy has just started to open up to the world, and it has great potential to grow.

For the Greater Tokyo area — namely, Tokyo, Kanagawa, Chiba and Saitama — the Japan Real Estate Institute (JREI) has reported a steady increase in the home price indices in the past few years. The index reached a high of 194.3 in 1993 before dropping steadily to 76.44 at the end of 2012. From the start of 2013, the index has generally been on the uptrend, rising to 90.43 in April 2017. However, the index remains at less than half of the 1993 peak.

Looking forward, we expect the index to continue its upward march.

Population Growth

Japan, like all developed nations, is faced with an ageing population. However, various policy measures introduced by Prime Minister Abe has been opening Japan to the world. We expect the population to grow. Here are the reasons why:

- Japan, known for its top quality education, produces many innovations and patents each year. Her universities and research laboratories have produced dozens of renowned Nobel laureates and they attract many foreign students a year. Within the last four years, two dozen universities started to offer undergraduate and postgraduate degree programmes that are delivered in English. This, alongside the very affordable school fees (starting from as low as S$7,000 a year) attracted students all over the English-speaking world. At the end of 2016, there were 239,287 international students in Japan. As the number of degree programmes that are offered in English increased, the number of international students climbed. The Japan Ministry of Education set a target for the total number of incoming international students to reach 300,000 each year. We are optimistic that the increase in international student population will increase demand for rental apartments.

Figure 1: Number of International Students in Japan

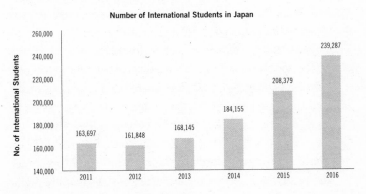

Number of International Students in Japan

Source: Japan Student Services Organization (JSSO), IPA

The increase in international students will also result in another benefit for Japan: raising the overall population count in the long term. With an increasing number of retirees leaving the workforce, together with an economy that continues to create new jobs, these students are likely to continue staying in Japan for work. It means a continued demand for housing even after they have graduated.

In fact, we have already assisted parents to purchase apartments near to the universities which their children are attending. We believe that this trend of home investments will grow stronger as more parents in Southeast Asia learn about the advantages of Japan's universities and know of the strength of the employment market.

- One of the strategies Prime Minister Abe adopted to boost the economy was to open Japan's doors to more foreign investments by promoting various industry sectors, such as healthcare, biotechnology and IT. One overarching aim was to attract foreign direct investments worth JPY35 trillion (about S$430 billion) by 2020. As a result, more jobs were created and, in order to meet the demand from Japanese and foreign multi-national companies, employment pass restrictions were relaxed for high-skilled workers from all over the world to fill the job vacancies.

Since the middle of 2016, the total number of job vacancies in Japan has maintained at well above the 900,000 mark. The abundance of jobs in the major cities attracted both Japanese workers from smaller cities and foreigners. And to encourage more foreigners to live and work in Japan for the long term, the length of time a foreigner needs to stay in Japan to qualify to be a Permanent Resident can be as short as a year. As a result, cities like Tokyo and Osaka have been seeing population gains, which translates to an increased demand for housing. No surprises that the rental market has also improved steadily.

Tourism

Japan, one of the favourite destinations for global travellers, is expecting a multi-year boom in its tourism industry. Rugby World Cup 2019, Tokyo Olympics 2020, 2020 Robot Olympics, Asian Games 2026 are just a few of the major international sports events that will be staged in Japan.

On top of that, in December 2016, the parliament passed the bill legalising casinos. Many of the leading gaming operators from the U.S., Macau, etc, have already expressed their interest in gaining a foothold in this lucrative market. It is likely for the first integrated resort to be built by the early 2020s.

A relaxation of visitor visas was the major contributor to the tourism industry boom. Foreign visitor arrivals jumped from 10.3 million in 2013 to 24.0 million in 2016. This boom generated many jobs in the tourism sector and boosted property prices for segments such as retail, hotels and serviced apartments. The current number of hotel rooms in major gateway cities is forecast to be insufficient to cater to the huge influx of tourists. The shortage of hotel rooms and serviced apartments is partly alleviated by home sharing schemes. And this, we believe will add to the increased demand for residential properties.

Stronger Economy

As the economy grows and the labour market expands, it is hoped that the higher disposable income of the salaried workers in Japan will translate to higher consumption. To make up for the shrinking labour force due to ageing population, Prime Minister Abe has strongly pushed for women to enter the workforce and relaxed the conditions for foreigners to be employed in Japan.

This will affect the real estate markets in a few ways. The increased disposable income will push up rental budgets, and couples with dual income will seek to upgrade their homes. As the demand for residences increases, the value of these properties will increase as well.

Figure 2: Total Number of Foreigners Residing in Japan

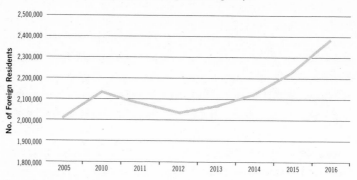

Total Number of Foreigners Residing in Japan

Source: Ministry of Justice (MOJ) Japan, IPA

These structural changes that we see in Japan are not new to us in Singapore. In the aftermath of the dotcom crash and the outbreak of SARS, Singapore undertook a bold move to open up its economy further: promoting the education sector to foreign students, encouraging immigration, boosting tourism jobs, introducing two casinos and opening up the banking sector and the services industry. The decade from 2003 to 2013, which included a severe global financial crisis, saw our private residential price index gain more than 100%.

In Japan, and particularly in Tokyo, the residential price boom has just begun.

A Note about the Fee to Buyer's Broker

I often get asked about a market practice in Japan, where the buyer pays fees to the buyer's broker and the seller pays fees to the seller's broker.

We, together with our partners in Japan, represent Singapore buyers to invest in properties in Japan. As Singapore investors are not used to the practice of paying a buyer's fee of 3% of the transaction price, there is often a discussion involving the bargaining of the fees. For this and a few other reasons, most Japanese sellers and brokers prefer to sell to Japanese investors as they know the market practices well.

In my experience working with various Japanese partners over the last five years, they have sometimes specifically requested me not to disclose certain opportunities to investors who are not familiar with Japanese customs and practice. We have lost a few attractive deals to HongKong-ers, Chinese and Taiwanese investors, who are able to make quick decisions and are willing to pay the standard commissions to their brokers.

In Japan, the brokers representing buyers and sellers carry a lot more responsibilities compared to their counterpart in Singapore. Singapore being under the British law system has conveyancing lawyers involved in property transactions, but there are none in Japan. About 90% of the due diligence with various government departments — the background checks of the asset and the owners, the encumbrances, the verification of documents, etc. — are all done by the brokers representing the buyer or the seller. The only legal practitioner involved in the transaction is a "judicial scrivener", whose main responsibility is to register or de-register the title of the land and the building for the seller, the buyer and the lenders at the government title registry on the final settlement day.

Another point to keep in mind is that the brokers in Japan may want to limit the good investment opportunities only to Japanese buyers because they will get to earn the 3% buyer's fee in full. When offering the opportunities to Singapore investors through my agency in Singapore, the Japanese brokers are earning only half the fees — they have to share the 3% buyer's fee with my company — and are therefore less motivated to reach out to Singapore investors.

I would like to assure readers that if you want to invest in Japan, the request from your representative broker for a 3% buyer's fee is a common market practice in Japan, which is in line with property transaction regulations stipulated by the Japanese government.

For those who are keen to participate in the rising Japanese real estate market, you may familiarise yourselves looking through a few of the many websites, which explain the brokerage fees in Japan:

- http://japanpropertycentral.com/real-estate-faq/real-estate-brokerage-fees-in-japan/
- http://www.propertyjapan.sg/ownership-costs/
- http://global.sumitomo-res.com/flow/
- http://www.realestate-tokyo.com/sale/guide/property-buying-cost-taxes/
- http://japanpropertycentral.com/real-estate-faq/purchase-costs-when-buying-real-estate-in-japan/

So if you see an attractive opportunity, follow what Japanese investors do and pay the 3% buyer's fee to the broker representing you in the transaction. Happy investing!

26. Why Not Malaysia?

12 August 2016, TODAY

Singapore and Malaysia signed off on a Memorandum of Understanding on 19 July 2016 to build a High Speed Rail (HSR) linking Singapore and Kuala Lumpur. In the meeting between the two prime ministers in 2015, it was recognised that the much hyped-up target year of 2020 was unrealistic and Prime Minister Najib explained that the overall implantation would take at least seven years, hinting at a revised target completion year of 2022. Finally, with the signing of the memorandum, we get the long-awaited update on this matter with a more reasonable target completion year of 2026.

Inter-city and international railway projects are never simple, and deadlines get postponed all the time. Acquiring land across four Malaysian states, resettling affected families and businesses and, most importantly, raising sufficient funds for the entire project will require a few more years, especially if local issues and politics disrupt the timeline.

The project is repeatedly hailed by both governments as a "game changer" for our economies. Yes, it can change the economic game for Singapore and for Kuala Lumpur, provided it is well executed, begin operations on schedule and, as Singaporeans may well appreciate, operates smoothly thereafter.

Fast acting investment advisors are already spouting the economic benefits of the HSR and recommending various types of investments all over Peninsula Malaysia. However, to consider whether the HSR will change the game for the whole of Peninsula Malaysia, outside of Kuala Lumpur, we have to look deeper.

Dr Qin Yu, an assistant professor of the National University of Singapore, authored a paper titled "No County Left Behind? The distributional impact of High-Speed Rail Upgrades in China". She concluded that "the reduction of transport costs for people between large cities may divert economic activities from counties to populous urban districts". The paper, already accepted and awaiting publication by the Journal of Economic Geography, also revealed that the major cities which host the termini stations fare better, while the counties along the route of the high-speed rail saw 3–5% declines in annual GDP arising from a reduction of 9–11% in Fixed Asset Investments.

If findings from this study were applicable to the Singapore-Malaysia HSR, we could expect to see the economies of Singapore and Kuala Lumpur expand while the economies around the six intermediate stations shrink: Putra Jaya, Seremban, Ayer Keroh, Muar, Batu Pahat and Nusajaya. For the cities and towns such as Port Dickson, Tampin and Kluang which are bypassed, the economic outlook might be even more dire.

Residents of Kuala Lumpur, Seremban and Malacca will find it a breeze to work in Singapore via daily commuting, earning incomes in Singapore dollars, while returning home every evening to be with their families. There could be further "brain-drain" or "skills-drain" from various Malaysian cities to Singapore.

Malaysia My Second Home (MM2H) Program

The programme started in 2002 and a total of 29,814 applicants have been approved since. The current total number of participants could be lower as there may be double counting in cases of renewals and there could also be dropouts along the way.

In the first four months of 2016, approvals were given to 424 applicants, meaning that on an annualised basis we might expect a total of about 1,300 approved applicants this year, or a drop of about 40% from 2015 (which itself saw a drop of 28% from 2014).

Figure 1: Approval Statistics for Malaysia My Second Home Program since Inception

Year	No. of Participants Approved	Total No. of Partipants Approved	Y-O-Y Change (%)
2002	818	818	-
2003	1,645	2,463	101.1
2004	1,917	4,380	16.5
2005	2,615	6,995	36.4
2006	1,729	8,724	−33.9
2007	1,503	10,227	−13.1
2008	1,512	11,739	0.6
2009	1,578	13,317	4.4
2010	1,499	14,816	−5.0
2011	2,387	17,203	59.2
2012	3,227	20,430	35.2
2013	3,675	24,105	13.9
2014	3,074	27,179	−16.4
2015	2,211	29,390	−28.1
2016 (April)	424	29,814	−80.8
Total	29,814	29,814	−

Source: http://mm2h.gov.my/index.php/en/home/programme/statistics

Compared with Singapore's objectives, as stated in the January 2013 Population White Paper — which grants citizenship status to about 15,000–25,000 Permanent Residents, and Permanent Residency status to 30,000 foreigners and every year — the MM2H programme does not look popular.

Amongst the approved MM2H applicants are Singaporeans who have applied for the MM2H status in order to enjoy the privilege of buying cars at a discount for their relatives who reside in Malaysia. Each approved MM2H person is entitled to purchase "one new motor car made or assembled in Malaysia" with an exemption from excise duties, thus saving tens of thousands of Ringgit for their families.

The cumulative 29,814 applicants added a mere 0.1% to the 30 million population of Malaysia. Even if all the approved participants chose to reside in Iskandar, they will only fill up 10 percent of the 300,000 residential units launched in the last five years. There is no data indicating whether the MM2H participants contribute significantly to the Malaysian economy or to the investments and rental of residential properties. Based on the information presented above, I am inclined to conclude that the 13-year-old MM2H Program has a negligible impact on both the economy and the demand for property.

Iskandar's Promise and Letdown

Closer to Singapore, pundits continue to sing praises about the growth potential of Iskandar. In a drive around Nusajaya in early July, we observed that the pace of construction seemed slow, as several projects that were fully sold years ago remain under construction.

One large billboard proclaimed "Akan Datang" and "Coming Soon" above a construction site hoarding for a luxury condominium project which failed to launch after the 2013 peak of the Iskandar hype. Needless to say, construction has not started.

As for the completed condominiums, banners displaying "For Sale" and "For Rent" are commonplace. A casual count estimates that about 10% of the apartments are furnished with curtains. Bare electrical wires dangling from the ceilings of balconies reflect the "never-occupied" state of the many apartments.

A medical centre that was launched with much fanfare was opened for business in late 2015. As of July 2016, no more than a quarter of the clinics in the medical centre has been taken up by specialist doctors.

Refunds and Backing Out of Iskandar

Some developers in Iskandar have dropped prices by more than 15% to move leftover apartments, adding downward pressure on valuations. Buyers who took deferred payment plans and paid down less than 10% of purchase prices are walking away from their investments. Some investors have gone further, requesting developers to refund their down payments by citing the inability to secure mortgages as the banks have tightened up on loans to foreigners.

The situation with commercial and industrial properties is similar. While millions of square feet of commercial and industrial space are completed and waiting for tenants, several high-profile projects have never broken ground.

We have scant information about the value of investments into Iskandar. In particular, how investments into businesses and factories that will create jobs. Of the much quoted RM$202 billion invested into Iskandar between 2006 to March 2016, how much was for the reclamation of land and for the purchase of land by developers? How much was due to the sales of strata-titled apartments, SOHOs, offices and industrial space by the same developers? What is the value that is double counted in the real estate industry? What about the value of investments that were withdrawn or cancelled?

Conclusion

Malaysia held promise until over development and over-hyped promises propelled valuations to the stratosphere, especially when Iskandar prices matched those in prime Kuala Lumpur districts. Investments from Singapore are unlikely to increase given the slump in trade, manufacturing and financial services, while corporate default risks are rising.

I am eager to be the first to upgrade my call on Malaysian

properties to a "Buy". However, against an uncertain political leadership and economic outlook, which could depress real estate valuations or weaken the ringgit versus the Singapore dollar, my call on Malaysia real estate is an "Avoid" for now.

Author's Note

This article appeared in *TODAY* paper with the title *Avoid Malaysian Property, Especially Iskandar*. It drew a lot of criticisms, especially from investors and property agents who have stakes in Iskandar projects. There was even a threat of a lawsuit. A year later, as I edit this article for inclusion into the book, I reflect on the call made last year and I am satisfied that the call is appropriate: Malaysia's real estate market remains oversupplied.

27. Focus on Regional Bread-and-Butter Housing Products

27 June 2016, The Edge Property

As market conditions in Singapore worsened progressively since the start of 2014, many developers from Singapore ventured overseas. No surprises that most would start with markets that they feel they know well: England, Australia, Malaysia and China. A few ventured into relatively newer markets for Singapore companies, such as Cambodia and Japan. And a few large-sized Singapore developers rekindled their property development activities in Vietnam and Indonesia after some years of hiatus.

Almost every developer that went overseas have planted their flags in the middle-to-high-end residential segments of the cities they chose. And some are now realising that there are not enough buyers for skyscraping luxury condominiums, for example in Malaysia, Cambodia, Vietnam and Australia.

It is probably coincidental that they all chose the same segment of the property market in the various countries. However, I do wonder whether they have considered a segment of the market that is much bigger and where demand will outpace supply for the next 15 years. I am pointing to the affordable housing segment in markets such as Cambodia, Indonesia, Myanmar and Vietnam.

But why have the Singapore developers not dipped their toes in the affordable housing segment? We can clearly learn from the successful example of HDB's towns where 80% of Singapore families are sheltered.

It seems that developers from Singapore have an aversion to building cheap housing overseas. Developers may not want to be associated with a segment that is perceived to have a stigma and which may look unglamorous. They may also be under the impression that the margins are thin, government laws for affordable housing unclear and dismiss the segment with "anyway, it is the government's job to provide housing for the masses".

Let the Numbers Do the Talking

Figure 1: GDP and population data of ASEAN member countries and the immediate shortage of housing supply

	GDP per capita* (US$ in 2014)	Population in 2014*	Population forecast 2030 ~	Estimates for number of homes to be built
Cambodia	1,094.60	15,328,000	19,603,000	1.1 million new homes needed between 2015 to 2030
Indonesia	3,491.90	254,455,000	303,430,000	Backlog of 13.5 million homes and President Jokowi set a target to build 10 million homes by 2019.
Myanmar	1,203.80	53,437,000	61,634,000	Yangon city itself needs 170,000 homes per year due to population growth and domestic migration till 2030
Vietnam	2,052.30	90,729,000	105,367,000	374,000 additional homes per year till 2040

Sources:

* data.worldbank.org

~ United Nations Department of Economic and Social Affairs, Population Division, "World Population Prospects, the 2015 Revision"

http://www.akp.gov.kh/?p=69417

http://www.antaranews.com/en/news/98557/indonesia-to-start-implementation-of-one-million-houses-program

http://frontiermyanmar.net/en/news/ministry-seeks-foreign-partners-low-cost-housing

World Bank report: "Vietnam Affordable Housing — A Way Forward", October 2015

As shown in Figure 1, the governments of Cambodia, Indonesia, Myanmar and Vietnam have estimated their needs for a total of about 2 million new homes per year. To bring things into perspective, as a comparison, HDB in its over 50 years of history has built about 1.1 million dwelling units in Singapore. Therefore, the potential for Singapore's developers to build mass affordable housing in our neighbouring markets is huge!

A company called National Housing Organization (NHO) had a stellar start in Vietnam, developing about 5,000 affordable housing units in the last four years. Mr Tan Tee Keon, a Malaysian investor who co-founded the company, successfully adapted the lessons from affordable housing projects in Thailand and Singapore, to mid-scale projects of around a thousand apartments each in Hanoi, Danang and Ho Chi Minh City.

With the World Bank and the Vietnamese government estimating that they need another 374,000 dwelling units per year until 2040 — and most of the demand concentrated in the mass affordable category around major cities and industrial parks — it looks like NHO has a very long term, stable and sustainable business in Vietnam.

Even Better, There Are Formulas to Follow

In the four countries we are discussing, the United Nations estimated that their total population will increase by about 77 million by the year 2030. So there is no denying that the market demand will continue to grow. But how do we even begin to tap into this vast market of home buyers?

Amazingly, there is actually a rule of thumb for developing affordable housing. And we know how Singaporeans love formulas, don't we?

While we know that demand for affordable housing is very high, we have to note that the buyers' ability to pay is limited by their household income. The general guideline is to appropriately size and price the houses or the apartments at no more than three times the annual household income of the target buyers. As an example, a developer planning such a project around the fringes of Bandung City in West Java could reference the minimum wage guidelines of about S$250 per month, multiply that by 36 months and then double it for a young couple, to derive a selling price of S$18,000 for the homes. Developers targeting households comprising university graduates may price their homes starting from S$36,000 as graduates who get married at around 24–25 years of age generally earn over S$500 per person per month.

Based on the selling price, investors should then select reasonably priced sites and manage the construction costs tightly in order to enjoy modest profit margins, backed by the potential of large transaction volumes.

Recommendation

This is my message for developers venturing outside of Singapore: there are abundant long-term opportunities to develop mass market, affordable housing within ASEAN for as little capital as say, S$5 million. We will be able to do well as we are satisfying the hunger for comfortable housing by supplying "bread and butter", while the high-end market is oversupplied with foie gras and truffles.

We might take a leaf from the books of Hong Kong. While the Hong Kong residential market has set world records for prices of luxury housing time and again, as an advanced economy and a global financial centre, many residents cannot afford a comfortable night's rest. There is a lack of affordable housing in a first world city such as Hong Kong where the younger and middle-lower income families need to save 20 years of salaries to buy their first homes.

The real estate development world will herd towards mass affordable housing. Salted egg is already the new truffle. Singaporean developers should lead that charge.

ABOUT THE AUTHOR

 Ku Swee Yong is the CEO and Key Executive Officer of International Property Advisor Pte Ltd as well as a co-founder of HugProperty. com. From November 2013 to November 2016, he was concurrently the CEO of Century 21 Singapore. Prior to running his own practice, he was a Director in the Real Estate Centre of Expertise at Société Générale Private Banking, responsible for advising clients on real estate investments, the Director of Marketing and Business Development at Savills Singapore and the General Manager at Far East Organization's Indonesia office.

He holds an MBA in Marketing from University of Hull, UK, and completed his BSc in the Imperial College, University of London, UK and the Institut Louis Pasteur, Université de Strasbourg, France.

Swee Yong's opinion is regularly featured in the *Straits Times*, *Business Times*, 新明日报, 联合早报, *Channel NewsAsia*, *TODAY*, etc. He has published four books on the property market: *Real Estate Riches*, *Building Your Real Estate Riches*, *Real Estate Realities* and *Weathering a Property Downturn*.

He is among a rare few property agents who has been appointed as a part-time lecturer in both the Department of Real Estate in the National University of Singapore and the School of Design and Environment in Ngee Ann Polytechnic.

OTHER BOOKS BY THE AUTHOR

REAL ESTATE RICHES

*Understanding Singapore's Property Market
in a Volatile Economy*
ISBN 978-981-4346-51-1

If you're looking to buy a property in Singapore, whether to live in, lease out, or sell, this book is the essential guide to help you understand the property market and the factors that can affect your investment. The collection of articles presented address many common questions that real estate investors ask and give a succinct overview of the property landscape. They also clarify government policies, dispel common misconceptions and put into perspective the factors to consider when buying property. Commentaries provide further insights into the local property scene.

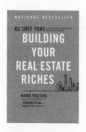

BUILDING YOUR REAL ESTATE RICHES

*Hard Truths about Singapore's Commercial
and Residential Markets*
ISBN 978-981-4382-06-9

Following the success of Real Estate Riches, property expert Ku Swee Yong offers another essential guide to help investors maximise their investment returns. Backed by solid research and astute observations, this book cuts through the haze of speculation and advertising clutter. Focusing on commercial, industrial and residential properties, the author reveals new insights in never-before-published data and addresses current issues faced by property investors through a collection of articles previous published in *TODAY*, *The Business Times* and *Forbes Indonesia* magazine.

REAL ESTATE REALITIES

Accommodating the Investment
Needs of Today's Society
ISBN 978-981-4516-39-6

Property expert Ku Swee Yong offers an updated essential guide to help investors protect their investment capital. This book cuts through the haze of speculation and advertising clutter and is backed by solid research and astute observations. While the focus is on Singapore's real estate, the author also shares his views on overseas markets such as UK, Japan, Australia, Cambodia and the Iskandar region of Johor. Readers will benefit from new insights in never-before-published data about Singapore's MasterPlan 2014.

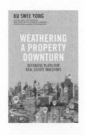

WEATHERING A PROPERTY DOWNTURN

Defensive Plays for
Real Estate Investors
ISBN 978-981-4751-06-3

Ku Swee Yong's books have become valuable resources for property investors in Singapore over the past few years. In this book, he takes stock of the prolonged downturn and weak market conditions and offers useful defensive strategies in the face of supply gluts and weakening prices. The lead article warns of potential risks arising from an extremely high rate of home ownership in Singapore, followed by frank insights into local property segments. The book also includes illuminating coverage on some regional markets which he recommends investors to look into.